✦ ✦ ✦ Poetry and Society

Poetry and Society

THE ROLE OF POETRY IN
ANCIENT GREECE

———

BRUNO SNELL

———

Indiana University Press

Bloomington

1961

PREFACE

THE PRESIDENT and Board of Trustees of Indiana University
in Bloomington kindly invited me to deliver the twenty first
series of lectures sponsored by the Patten Foundation in
March and April of 1960. I gratefully accepted this invitation,
and my special thanks are due to the Chairman of the Patten
Foundation Committee, Professor John M. Mueller.

In giving these lectures the form of a book, nothing has
been basically altered; although many points might have
been elaborated more carefully and illustrated by more extensive documentation. Further references to modern literature also might have made it easier for the reader to find
more information and to see where certain opinions have
previously been formulated. To the works of Hermann
Fränkel (*Dichtung und Philosophie des frühen Griechen-
tums,* New York, 1951; *Wege und Formen Frühgriechischen
Denkens,* München, 1955) and E. R. Dodds (*The Greeks
and the Irrational,* University of California Press, 1951) I

owe more than I could possibly tell an audience without talk-
ing footnotes. At first I tried to make a scholarly book out of
this publication but I soon realized that to do so would in-
volve changing its whole composition and texture.

For much help, especially for editing my English, I thank
Professor Frederick L. Beaty of the English Department at
Indiana University. Professor Norman T. Pratt, Jr., has carefully looked through my manuscript and has given me his
advice not only on niceties of style and idiom but on many
points of substance. I shared a rare experience of hospitality
and friendship during the six weeks of my stay in Bloomington, when Professor Pratt and Professor S. Palmer Bovie gave
me the opportunity to discuss in leisurely fashion our common interests.

Special thanks I owe to two friends I had the pleasure of
meeting again—the President of Indiana University, Dr.
Herman B Wells, and Professor Horst Frenz. Without further
words they themselves know best why I am deeply grateful
to them.

BRUNO SNELL

Bloomington, Indiana
April 11, 1960

BIBLIOGRAPHICAL NOTE

Sappho and Alcaeus are quoted from: *Poetarum Lesbiorum Fragmenta
ediderunt Edgar Lobel et Denys Page*, Oxford, 1955.

The fragments of Greek tragedians are from: *Tragicorum Graecorum
Fragmenta rec. Aug. Nauck, editio secunda*, Leipzig, 1889.

The fragments of lyrical poets (except Sappho and Alcaeus), i.e., Archilochus, Alcman, Simonides, etc., are from: *Anthologia Lyrica Graeca ed. E.
Diehl, editio altera*, Leipzig 1936–1942; fasc. 1, editio tertia, Leipzig, 1949.

CONTENTS

❖ ❖ ❖

1: Poetry and Society, 1

2: Homer, 12

3: Early Archaic Lyric Poetry, 28

4: Late Archaic Lyric Poetry, 49

5: Tragedy, 72

6: Comedy and Hellenistic Poetry, 91

Index, 113

✥ ✥ ✥   Poetry and Society

I

POETRY AND SOCIETY

❖ ❖ ❖

POETRY is influenced by social conditions.[1] It is, moreover, a mirror for social conditions, as for life and emotions.[2] But in ancient Greece it was more. Poetry was a forerunner of philosophical, political, and sociological thinking. Poetry acquired sufficient status to become a determinant of social forms, a guide in political experimentation, an innovator in language, a catalyst in the evolution of Greece from a primitive to a sophisticated society.

Poetry: forerunner of thought and change. In exploring this theme we may ask what possibilities for social behavior existed in the consciousness of men in different ages; and

1. The question—how society at any time influenced form and subject-matter in poetry—stands in the center of Marxist historical research, and, aside from historical materialism, deserves thorough investigation.

2. If we asked ourselves how the poets represented the social conditions of their time, we would take up a theme that M. I. Finley has treated in his illuminating book on *The World of Odysseus*. Inevitably comedy would come to the foreground and we should be obliged to treat the subjects discussed by Victor Ehrenberg in his book, *The People of Aristophanes*.

1

further, to what extent men at any time were aware of the forms in which they could bind themselves to one another. In our time such consciousness is found in sociological theories, where it is usually connected with social programs. Such theories and programs existed in Greece as early as the time of the Sophists. However, long before man embarked upon such reflections he, of course, had certain notions about the foundation on which human society rests, and perhaps it will turn out that important aspects of later social theories cannot be understood unless one knows something about earlier antiquity.

From the centuries preceding the Sophists—that is, prior to the second half of the fifth century before Christ—hardly anything has been preserved except poetry: first the epics of Homer and Hesiod, then lyric poetry, and finally in the fifth century the tragedies. Only the poets teach us how the Greeks lived together and what they thought about society. Hence, if the social consciousness of the early Greeks is to be discussed, the sources themselves are responsible for the fact that the subject of this book is poetry and society.

The poets from Homer to the tragedians not only reflected the viewpoints prevailing in their time and in their social class (for they were not just representatives of particular groups), but they contributed in diverse ways to the development of new ideas on the manner in which men can live together. It will be difficult to decide how far the poets in particular instances say something conventional or new; and it is not here proposed to enter into the philosophical question which is suggested at this point—whether society influences the poet more than the poet influences society—which is perhaps not unlike the hackneyed question: "Which came first, the chicken or the egg?"

Today we are bound to other human beings by a multitude of social groups in which we have membership. There is the family, the state, the profession; there are religious organizations and political parties; there are clubs and associations for the cultivation of common interests; there are personal relationships, and so on. Some of these links are very ancient; others have evolved in the course of history. Hence arises the fascinating question as to how old ties lose their importance and new ones emerge. Indeed it was in early Greece that a significant change took place. However, what developed there can be understood only after we have asked a very fundamental question: how a man stood in relation to his fellow men.

Originally man had a definite social function. When did it occur and how did it happen that man can also feel lonely in society? That he can suffer in his environment? That it can become so alien to him that he may desire to change it?

Since we are dealing with poetry, perhaps we should ask: when did the idea first appear that a poet seeks loneliness in order to give free rein to his thoughts and feelings? In antiquity was there someone like Petrarch who withdrew to Vaucluse, or like Jacques in Shakespeare's *As You Like It*, who fled from the hustle and bustle of mankind and who "sucked melancholy out of a song, as a weasel sucks eggs"? Did the poets of antiquity imagine a social order in which there would be fewer hardships and sufferings? Did they also try to reform the existing order of society?

We do not want to pursue social conditions or sociological theories for themselves but rather the possibilities of social behavior and the awareness men have had at any time of how they were bound to their fellow men. We do not accept the explanation that history has in store certain fixed forms of possible societies, and that certain of these forms come into prominence at one time or another. We suggest that man—especially in Greece—first had to acquire the intellectual hypotheses for many of the forms of society.

Let us begin with a consideration of how in the earliest Greek period, that is, in the time of Homer, men had a feeling of belonging together, to what extent a man could be in concord or discord with his fellow men, whom he called his friend and whom his foe, and so on. It will certainly become obvious that the conceptions of those early days differ considerably from those which we find in classical times or those with which we are now familiar.

We shall not be able to manage this altogether without some philological discussion of the meaning of single Homeric words. To give an example, the words *philos* and *echthrós,* which we usually translate as "friend" and "enemy," have, as will be shown, markedly different meanings in Homer.

Further, I shall try to trace how new themes came into being. Then the question arises whether this change points in a definite direction. In spite of recent scepticism over the naive and optimistic confidence of the eighteenth century in "progress" and "development," numerous facts seem to substantiate that we have a uniform process before us—a most fascinating process—and step by step the rich human relations of a differentiated society develop. A radical transformation of mankind took place—a transformation which belongs to the historical phenomenon that one can designate as the discovery of the mind.

The oldest speculation on this subject, that higher civilization depends on the ability of men to live together, is found in the ninth book of the *Odyssey,* where Odysseus tells about his trip to the cultureless *Cyclopes* (9.106ff.) :

And we came to the land of the Cyclopes, a fierce, uncivilized people, who never lift a hand to plant or plough but put their trust in the Gods. All the crops they require spring up unsown and untilled. . . . The Cyclopes have no assemblies for their deliberations, nor any settled customs, but live in hollow caverns in the mountain heights, where each man is lawgiver to his children and his wives, and nobody cares a jot for his neighbours [translated by E. V. Rieu].

This contrast shows that in the poet's mind it is a sign of human culture to consult in the assembly, in the market place, and decide jointly what "right" is, so that every man does not govern his household according to his own arbitrary will. Now this does not mean that Homer's time was acquainted with a codified law that determined in every case what would or would not be allowed. Certainly many a passage in Homer's epics shows that quarrels could be settled by discussion, arbitration, and judgment; but an awareness of a valid and binding obligatory law, holding human society together and determining the actions of individuals, did not as yet exist. Traditional usage and convention rule community life; and when a dispute arises, men are helped by a storehouse of experience and by recollection of similar cases, but not by a law that has been carefully thought out and based on general principles. That is why the prestige of old Nestor, who has seen three generations, is so great among his fellow heroes and why they listen so willingly to his lengthy discourses.

When the Greeks move against Troy, they undoubtedly want to rectify the injustice that Paris did to Menelaos by robbing him of his wife, Helen. But such a justification of the war is hardly mentioned. When Achilles is angry with Agamemnon for taking the maiden Briseis away from him, he is furious more because his honor has been insulted than because something illegal or unjust has befallen him. He feels insulted that Agamemnon does such a thing to him, the strongest and most splendid of heroes. The issue is not that he, a simple man, has been deceived and dealt with unjustly. Along with the primitive, peasant egoism that directs the attention of Homer's characters to the possession of cattle, property, and treasures, there is a higher, more chivalric egoism, in which a man's honor is his most priceless possession. But more exalted common interests like justice, state, social responsibility have only a dim existence in the theoretical consciousness, even though effective and practical moral restraint exists, especially in inherited traditions.

People become conscious of their city, their homeland, when it is in danger and must be defended. It is not an abstract state one has to stand up for; on the contrary, something very concrete is at stake. Then men have to help and protect one another and see to it that possessions are not stolen and that women and children are not dragged away into slavery. However, when Paris, because he had abducted Helen, brought the Greeks against Troy and thereby jeopardized the city, Hector could reproach him for having really deserved to be stoned [3]—thus advocating ancient lynch-justice; yet there was no valid and effective judiciary standard to protect the community in such cases. Nestor says: [4] "He who finds pleasure in a terrible war among his own people stands outside his clan, his phratry [he is *aphrētōr*] and outside the conventional order of law [he is *athémistos*];" these are traditional ties but not institutions created out of deliberation. There is something else to be noticed: the authority of these traditional ties is in most cases connected with certain people, whose

3. *Iliad*, 3. 46ff.
4. *Iliad*, 9. 63.

duty it is to guard them; this is particularly true of kings and priests. In Homeric times there survived many reminiscences of the fact that power was ascribed to certain objects, as, for example, to a sceptre, to put men into orderly relationship. But such beliefs were no longer really effective.

The solidity of these early societies was based, of course, on religious convictions. In the same way, contracts between individuals and groups gained security because they were founded on a religious oath. Thus Hector, shortly before the battle in which he is killed, can request of Achilles that they bind themselves by an oath promising that the victor will honorably surrender the body of the vanquished. However, Achilles answers: [5]

Hector, argue me no agreements. I cannot forgive you. As there are no trustworthy oaths between men and lions, nor wolves and lambs have spirit that can be brought to agreement, but forever these hold feelings of hate for each other, so there can be no love between you and me, nor shall there be oaths between us . . . [translated by Richard Lattimore].

Even in ties that are least binding there is obviously a divine guidance. In any case, whereas we say "birds of a feather flock together," Homer says: [6] "As a god always causes those who are similar to associate with one another."

If in this way cultic and religious considerations determine the social order, one may ask whether—besides these factors or in addition to them—personal motives deserve to be spoken of. Just as in the political sphere abstract law is not seen in its true nature; so in the sphere of domestic and private life, human feelings do not appear as the expression of the soul.

5. *Iliad,* 22. 260ff.
6. *Odyssey,* 17. 218

Marriage is an institution consecrated by tradition. A husband can love his wife because of her beauty or her other virtues; and when they are separated from one another, they can yearn for each other, as Odysseus longs for Penelope. But a spiritual sense of belonging to each other is nowhere in Homer described or motivated. One can be especially friendly with someone, as Achilles is with Patroclus; but an inner spiritual union is never stressed. They together can be useful to friends and harmful to enemies, and thus practically and actively stand together. No one ever feels compelled to consider why he is especially bound to this individual or that one; this bond is at any time the result of established custom or the situation at hand. Obviously Odysseus and Penelope, Achilles and Patroclus provide a fair picture of the friendly and marital relationship, but the "inner" and the "spiritual" remain unmentioned, and not in order to make the characterization more objective, but because the linguistic means of expressing these qualities was not yet in existence.

The Homeric word for "love," "to be friendly with someone" (*phileîn*), does not mean a spiritual attachment but rather a friendly act. For that reason Odysseus (10. 14) can say that the king of the winds, Aeolus, "loved" him and his companions for a whole month—that is to say, hospitably entertained them. Thus "dear," or "friend" (*philos*), is applied to whoever pursues identical interests and has the same intentions. Even the parts of a man's body, which serve him in a friendly manner, are called "dear" or "loving." One lifts his dear arms up in a prayer to the gods, contemplates something in his dear heart, or lets food and drink slip down his dear throat. In these references the practical aspects are evident.

In several places in the *Iliad*, however, one notices how the meaning of the word grows out of this restricted reference.

When the delegation goes to Achilles in order to persuade him to forget his anger, Achilles replies (9. 335ff.) :

Agamemnon took Briseis away from me. And yes, we went to war in order to take back Helen, the wife of his brother. Are the sons of Atreus alone among mortal men the ones who love their wives? Since any who is a good man, and careful, loves her who is his own and cares for her, even as I now loved this one from my heart. . . . [*Ek thymoû phileon*, that is to say: I loved her with an inner impulse.]

Somewhat later (9. 480) Phoenix relates that he went as a fugitive to the father of Achilles: "who accepted me with a good will and gave me his love, even as a father loves his own son who is a single child brought up among many possessions . . . and, godlike Achilles, I made you all that you are now, and loved you out of my heart. . . ."

The special love, the heartfelt emotion, as we would say, is here expressed in two ways. First, it is the love which comes to Phoenix from Peleus, and which is shown by comparison with the love of a father, who is especially devoted to his only son, born in the autumn of his years. Then the love of Phoenix for Achilles is expressed with the same phrase used to describe Achilles' love for Briseis: "to love from the *thymos.*" "With inner impulse" shows that the individual can perceive his emotion as a particularly loving one; but Homer never says that men are knowingly bound together by the same feelings.

That a peculiar limitation lies in Homer's thought and language is due to the fact that he had quite a different idea of the human mind and spirit from that to which we are accustomed. Hermann Fränkel was the first to make the observation that Homer does not distinguish between body and soul.[7] *Soma,* the word that later means body, in Homeric language means corpse. *Psyche* is the breath of life that keeps a man alive and, after death, goes to Hades as a peculiar shade-like being. Besides *psyche,* Homer is acquainted with *noos,* a sort of inner eye with which a man can "see" or "perceive," somewhat in the sense of the phrase "I see, said the blind man." In addition, Homer is acquainted with *thymos,* mentioned previously, which is an inner organ that "stirs" a man—that is to say, conveys what we call passion or emotion—and also gives the impetus to physical movement.

The consequence of this conception of the soul is that Homer cannot express what we say in phrases like "feeling psychologically bound," "being intellectually of one mind," or "being spiritually in accord." From that it may be inferred that in the social life of Homer's time there were as yet no groups founded upon intellectual or spiritual unity.

It is evident that the social order is not independent of the possibilities which language provides. As civilization superimposes itself upon primitive living, nothing can be brought into being that has not previously been thought out—and that means formulated in speech.

Modern sociology and anthropology have from the beginning recognized how important it is to study primitive societies in order to understand modern society. In the initial stages of these studies, however, it was not clear how much the concepts of men and of community life differ in various parts of the world. Above all, one thing is important: we can become acquainted with the ideas of foreign peoples only when we receive them in the language in which they are originally expressed. At first, in order to acquire material for sociological research, questions were asked and answered with

7. *Göttinger gelehrte Anzeigen,* 1922, 193f.

the aid of interpreters, or else questionnaires were worked
out and distributed. It was not noticed that the questions
were based on suppositions that were not familiar to those
who answered, and for this reason could provoke only non-
sense—as though someone asked a child who as yet has not
learned mathematics what he thinks of the congruence of
triangles or the distribution of prime numbers. The only
person who can speak with authority about primitive societies
is the man who understands their language. Though they had
been forgotten, the ideas about language developed by Wil-
helm von Humboldt are again recognized and acknowledged
—namely, that language is not only an implement which
represents given objects, but that each language has a special
intellectual system in which each peculiarity is determined
by the whole.

In this connection the Greek language is of outstanding
importance because in our Western civilization the Greeks
through their own abilities made such remarkable progress
from a primitive to a sophisticated society; and the extant
authors serve as monuments to inform us of the various
stages of that development. The epics of Homer, which stand
at the beginning of European literature, reveal in many ways
a primitive spirit. They have a special value for us as compared with the documents of other primitive cultures. Because they could by no means have been influenced by modern thought that did not exist at the time, they are therefore
pure and unadulterated. Since beyond this they are great and
enduring poetry, they express this primitive world with
clarity and force.

2

HOMER

❖ ❖ ❖

Social relations in Homer are not looked upon as something created by human beings, say through a *contrat social*, but instead as something founded by the gods and handed down by tradition. This means that whatever ties bind men to one another are not the result of common intellectual convictions or common personal feelings. In friendship or love, for instance, feelings appear to be bound up with practical action and behavior in such a way that an individual treats another in a friendly or loving manner.

In the further evolution of Greek society two principal developments will be apparent: man through his own choice learns more and more to create new and original forms of living together; and the groups thus created are bound together by common intellectual interests or by mutual sentiments. This shows to what extent social life is dependent upon a new conception of the human mind that developed after Homer. For as long as the mind or soul was not yet thought of in its principal opposition to the body, mind could not be conceived as active or creative any more than it could be seen as a common mind linking together different people.

The Greek poets—first Homer, then the writers of lyric and dramatic poetry, and finally the Hellenistic poets—prepared the way for modern society. We can define this more precisely now. Step by step the Greek poets brought to light two elements of mind: first, its spontaneous activity; and second, its faculty of imparting itself to different individuals who were consequently linked together. Of course, the poets achieved this by virtue of their experiences with other men. They always learned anew that in spite of all traditions and convention they could feel a mutual sense of belonging with certain individuals who likewise felt this peculiar, individually discovered, mental unison. Once they had been expressed by poets, such new ideas could rapidly become public property and stamp their image on the social behavior of the entire community.

In Homer's epics we encounter a society held together by a fixed and uniform idea of what constitutes good and evil. The same values are esteemed by both Greeks and Trojans. Certainly there is no doubt about what a "good man," an *anèr agathós,* is, nor in what "virtue," *areté,* consists; and, in fact, these terms imply physical qualities and external success as well as moral excellence. Each man must be brave in war; he must be strong, tall, and handsome; he must be able to speak well and to give good counsel in the assembly; but in addition he must be rich and powerful. A perfect woman is expected to be beautiful, chaste, and experienced in all housework.

The more of such "virtues" an individual possesses, the more respect and honor accrue to him. The whole social system of the Homeric world is based on an awareness that these "virtues" are so easily recognized that everybody lays claim only to the share of honor appropriate to himself, while on the other hand a man confers upon others the honor rightfully belonging to them. This honor, *timé*, is something so well established that it can almost be measured: for instance, the value of a *geras,* a gift of honor that a hero receives when he is a guest, depends, so to speak, on the quantity of honor he possesses. Of course, conflicts can arise over these claims. In fact, the entire story of the *Iliad* is based upon the account of how Achilles' honor was insulted by Agamemnon's theft of Briseis and how the wrathful Achilles, by withdrawing from battle, brought all sufferings to the Greeks.

It is taken for granted by everyone in Homer's works that an individual who possesses no "virtue" cannot possibly receive "honor." Such a person has to serve those who do have "virtue." [1] This is especially applicable to the slaves, and we never hear in Homeric epics that anyone finds fault with this condition. However, if a free man like Thersites attempts to claim more esteem than he actually deserves by raising his voice and denouncing the "good people," that is considered impudent, and he is reprimanded with a sound whipping and derisive laughter.

In order that we may understand more precisely where in Homer's works the starting points for further development are to be found, let us consider the passages in which men are said by Homer to be "unanimous." As mentioned earlier, Homer cannot say that different people are of one mind, of one feeling, or of one mood. Yet the rudiments and intimations of this concept do exist.

Mental agreement can be explained by saying that two men

1. *Odyssey,* 15. 324; *Iliad,* 2. 188ff.

turn their minds toward a mutual goal. The union thus produced when two men ponder one and the same thing is seen not as a consolidation of minds but rather as a concerted effort directed toward a common objective. So instead of saying: "You have the same opinion that I have," Homer says: [2] "You consider the same thing that I consider," *ta gar phronéeis hát' egó per;* or instead of: "If we are unanimous," he says: [3] "If we give counsel along one and the same way," *ei dé pot' és ge mían bouleúsomen,* and so on. Of course, in such instances all that we call "mental" may be implied. This may be shown in the words of Thetis to her son Achilles, who comes to her in order to complain that Agamemnon has taken Briseis away from him: [4] "Why then Child, do you lament? What sorrow has come to your heart now? Tell me, do not hide it in your mind, and thus we shall both know."

The inner feeling of being bound together, or the sympathy in a common sorrow, is expressed by the desire to know the same thing. We shall encounter the same idea later in Sappho in a more highly developed state. But by then Sappho, as will be seen, can more fully express such unanimity.

But there is another phrase in Homer that seems to come even nearer to what we would call unanimity: *íson* or *héna thymòn échontes,* "having the same spirit," as we would say, or "having the same" or "having one *thymos,*" to use the Greek word. The use of this phrase is important and interesting. *Thymos* is the inner organ that stirs man. If Homer says that someone has a certain *thymos,* there is always an action involved. One can have a friendly or a hostile (*eúphrona, nēléa*) *thymos* toward someone else. Whoever has a weak or

2. E.g. *Iliad,* 4:361.
3. *Iliad,* 2. 379.
4. *Iliad,* 1. 363.

ineffectual *thymos* is a coward. Thus the phrase "having one" or "having the same *thymos*" is never used in situations in which two people share the same sorrow (as did Thetis and Achilles) or feel united in joy or have the same thoughts and convictions, but only when two people stand together in concerted action.

Twice in the *Iliad* the phrase "having the same *thymos*" is applied to the two Ajaxes. Homer says: [5] they would not withdraw from one another, but as two oxen "having the same *thymos*" draw the plow and sweat under the yoke, so these two took their stand in battle close to each other. Likewise Ajax the son of Telamon says to the son of Oileus: [6] "We who have the same *thymos* and bear the same name will fight against the Trojans and against Hector just as we heretofore have fought standing fast beside each other." Both times it is emphasized that they stand near one another and that they also form what virtually amounts to a bodily unit.

In these illustrations Homer says "having the same [*ison*] *thymos*;" in other instances in the *Iliad* we find "having one [*héna*] *thymos*." In the *Iliad* (17. 267), for example, we read:

The Trojans came down on them. . . ./As when at the outpouring place of a rain-glutted river/the huge surf of the sea roars against the current, out-jutting/beaches thunder aloud to the backwash of the salt-water,/with such a bellow the Trojans came on, but now the Achaians/stood fast about the son of Menoitios, in a single courage/and fenced beneath their bronze-armed shields. . . .

"In a single courage," as Lattimore translates "having one *thymos*," the Greeks stood against the wild onslaught of the Trojans. The fence of their shields closes them up in their

5. *Iliad*, 13. 704.
6. *Iliad*, 17. 720.

external appearance. This passage will again be of interest to us later because Tyrtaios, the Spartan poet of war, takes it up. The solid order of the phalanx of Spartan hoplites develops still further the ideas laid down in these verses and later makes them of political importance.

A compact battle formation such as that of the Myrmidons is described in verses 210 and following in the sixteenth book:

And their ranks . . . pulled closer together./And as a man builds solid a wall with stones set close together/for the rampart of a high house keeping out the force of the winds, so close together were the helms and shields massive in the middle./For shield leaned on shield, helmet on helmet, man against man . . ./so dense were they formed on each other./And before them all were two men in their armour, Patroklos/and Automedon, both of them in one single fury. . . .

Here too Homer says: "having one *thymos*." Again, as in the passage about the two Ajaxes, we have two heroes who are unanimous in fighting.

In the thirteenth book of the *Iliad* Aineias assaults Idomeneus, who calls his friends for help: "/and all these, a single spirit within them/came and stood in their numbers and sloped their shields over his shoulders" (v.487f.). Here too unanimity in fighting presents itself in a close standing together behind the compact shelter of shields. Here too the Trojans press forward with great noise (v.472) like hunters and hounds advancing against a wild boar. But here the poet not only says that the Greeks have one *thymos,* but he adds that they have one *thymos* in the *phrenes*—that is, in the diaphragm or the central portion of the body, where the organs of perception were thought to be located. So here, more than in the other instances, Homer suggests that this unanimity is something "mental."

The fourth passage of the *Iliad* mentioning the "one *thymos*" is found in Book Fifteen, verse 710, but by being set in another frame of reference, the phrase takes on a different meaning:

Trojans and Achaeans fought against one another in close combat/. . . nor any longer/had patience for the volleys, exchanged from bows and javelins/but stood up close against each other, *matching their fury* [here the Greek text has: having one *thymos*],/and fought their battle with sharp hatchets and axes, with great swords and with leaf-headed pikes. . . .

Here "having one *thymos*" does not mean "being unanimous," as it does in the other instances. Here they fight *against* each other with one *thymos,* because they are inspired by the same wild rage. In the other instances it was always the Greeks who had "one *thymos,*" but here both Greeks and Trojans possess it. They have, as one might say with an Homeric simile, the *thymos* of a lion, which drives them to fight against each other.

Wherever having one *thymos* means being unanimous, we always have a well-defined single situation, a common action. It always applies—and this is also true of the phrase "having the same *thymos*"—to Greeks in combat. We shall see later that this idea of unanimity among warriors is further developed by Tyrtaios. The great difference between Homer's concept and that of the later Spartan poet is that Tyrtaios not only describes single actions in which this unity is achieved, but by his exhortations he tries to realize it as a perpetual virtue which, according to his belief, is the very foundation of the state. This subject will be treated later.

In the *Odyssey* we learn something new that does not exist in the *Iliad*. In the third book (127ff.) Nestor, when referring to himself and Odysseus, says:

In all those years, whether at the general assembly or in the council of the Kings, not once did Odysseus and I find ourselves speaking on opposite sides. Having one *thymos* in our *noos* and in our prudent judgment we laid down the policy for the successful conduct of the Argives' affairs [translated by E. V. Rieu].

Oúte potè . . . dícha bázomen . . ./all' héna thymòn échonte nóōi kai epíphroni boulêi/phrazómeth' Argéioisin, hópōs óch' árista génoito. If you can follow the Greek, you will notice how the language has exerted some pains to underscore the fact that both have always been unanimous in the assembly (*agorá*) and in the council (*boulé*); they spoke the same—that means they pursued the same objectives—and had the same *thymos* in their *noos* and their advice—that means they had the same personal emotions in their conceptions about what was to be done. They were not only stirred by the same inner force, but saw the same goal before them. Here the *thymos* and the *noos*, the two organs of the soul that originally were strictly separate, work together, and we see how the poet approaches a new conception of the whole soul. But since no single word by which he might have designated this conception was at that time in existence, he had to speak in a roundabout manner in order to express it.

There is another word in Homer for "being of one mind," that is *homóphron,* which literally means "being of one diaphragm." It occurs first in the *Iliad* (22. 263): "Wolves and lambs are not of one mind, but are evil-minded (*kakà phronéousi*) one against the other;" that is to say, they are enemies and not friends. The *Odyssey* uses two derivatives of this word: *homophrosýne,* "the state of being of one mind," and the verb *homophronéein,* "to be of one mind."

In the sixth book of the *Odyssey,* Odysseus offers his good wishes to Nausicaa (v.18off.) :

May the Gods grant you your heart's desire; may they give you a husband and a home, and the harmony that is so much to be desired, since there is nothing nobler or more admirable than when two people having the same mind keep house as man and wife, confounding their enemies and delighting their friends . . . [translated by E. V. Rieu].

Here too the Greek text seems rather long-winded, for where the translation speaks of "harmony," the original has *homophrosýne*—that is, something like "unity of inner disposition toward other people"—and then follows, as a kind of variation, "having the same inner disposition in their thoughts"—*homophronéonte noémasin.* Only with a certain effort can Odysseus utter something that we describe very easily as inner concordance. But this concept is something that goes beyond the conventional ideas of early times.

All these passages share the use of the phrases "having the same" or "one *thymos*," or "being *homophron*," as applied to men who are united by traditional and hallowed ties: by marriage, by assembly or council, by a military organization or a combat unit. But if the "unanimity" of these groups is stressed, it should be noted that individuals in a particular way fulfill the traditional sense of belonging to their own groups but that they do not originate new forms of social groups. A further point is that this unanimity appears only in connection with the idea that one has to stand together in order to harm the enemy and to benefit the friend. Whereas in the *Iliad* this standing together is determined by individual situations and therefore has more of a transient nature, in the *Odyssey* it stretches out over a longer period and tends to be more enduring. That holds good as well for the unanimity of Nestor and Odysseus as for the ideal spouses Odysseus spoke of before Nausicaa. In both epics, however, people are unanimous in action—not in contemplation or mere feeling.

In the fifteenth book of the *Odyssey* we find the plural of the word *homophrosýne* which occurred in the words of Odysseus to Nausicaa. Telemachos says to Peisistratos that the journey they have made together will lead them to still further "unanimities." Previously he had said: "We may well claim that our fathers' friendship makes a lasting bond between us. Besides which, we are of the same age." The friendship between the two young men is originally the friendship existing between host and guest, which was inherited from their fathers, but it has grown beyond that stage. The idea that the journey leads to further "unanimities" is a remarkably new thought in Homer. The plural shows that we are dealing here not merely with the same general disposition of the soul or with mental concordance; instead, the single reactions of the mind are congruent. But here, even more clearly than in the phrase "to love someone from the *thymos*," the awareness dawns that there may be something like a "hearty" friendship.

We have repeatedly seen how important in Homer the relationship of friend or enemy is in determining the social behavior of man. From the very beginning, however, I have tried to make clear that to be a friend and to love is not so much a matter of pure sentiment but is always bound up with an activity, with treating someone kindly. But who in Homer is *philos* (friend), and who is *echthrós* (enemy)? We have already observed that *philos* is applied to the person who belongs to someone else and who advances the other person's endeavors. *Echthrós,* on the other hand, is originally applied to the man who is "outside." At any rate, the most plausible

etymology connects the word with the preposition *ex*.
Wilamowitz [7] has shown that in early Greece men differentiated between those gods who protected home and family,
settlement and kinsmen, field and tribe, and those who
haunted the mountains outside man's immediate realm. In
our fairy tales the ungrubbed, untouched forest is the sinister
wilderness where witches and giants are threatening. In
Greece a god like Pan appears between the rocks in the heat
of midday, and there are kindred demons in abundance.

Modern anthropologists have found out that in many
primitive civilizations the first major differentiation is made
between men who belong to one's own community, who are
friends, and those who live outside one's own familiar dis-
trict. Whoever lives beyond the river or the forest or the
mountain is an enemy. The country outside, the untamed
wilderness, is called *eschatiá* by the early Greeks. This word,
too, like *echthrós,* is derived from the preposition *ex*. In this
wilderness "out there" the law of the wasteland rules: everyone is hostile to everyone else, just as animals are hostile to
one another, and there are no civilizing traditions and conventions. Only by becoming a "guest-friend" of someone can
a man from outside enter into the civilized existence of an
alien community. Who is friend or enemy is not dependent
upon personal feelings, sympathy, or antipathy but is determined in advance by external circumstances.

Once somebody is a friend of somebody else he cannot
prove his friendship by exchanging opinions or sentiments,
but he can do so, and in certain circumstances he has to do so,
by exchanging gifts. These presents are by no means small
gifts that receive their value only as tokens of a hearty feeling,
but precious gifts that can be shown as treasures which have

7. *Glaube der Hellenen,* 1, 155.

adequately honored the friend, the father-in-law, the suitor of the daughter, or the participant in another agreement. We have to take this into account in order to understand fully why the exchange of gifts plays, as Finley has shown in his book on the *Odyssey,* such an important role in Homeric society.

Where "mental" bonds are lacking, social life is all the more regulated by strict ceremonies and prescribed formalities. We are rather inclined to regard such external practices as superficial rituals, but in doing so we are unfair to those times that had not yet learned to distinguish between inherent meaning and external form. The family lives together according to sacred customs; the warriors go to war with certain rites; the guest-friend is entertained according to established methods; social life is regulated by prayers, sacrifices, and religious festivals. People belong together when they unite again and again in common prescribed actions.

It is surprising that in spite of these many shared experiences there are scarcely any words in the Homeric language to express such common actions. It is all the more remarkable since later Greek developed an abundant supply of words constructed with the preposition *syn* (meaning "together with") to denote that several people engage in a common activity. Some of these words survive in modern English—as, for instance, *symposium* (common drinking) and *sympathy* (common feeling). This type of compound is completely missing in the *Iliad.* One could perhaps mention the verbs *symmetídomai* and *symphrázomai,* "to consider together," "to discuss together," but since that would be quite unique for Homer, it might be better to explain these words by comparing them to the phrase already mentioned: "to give counsel in the same direction"; the *syn* would not denote the common

action but the direction to one point. Thus Homer can say
syn-trechein (composed of *syn-* and the verb for "to run"):
which does not mean "to run in common with somebody
else" but "to run together to a certain point," not to "*run
together*" but "*to run together*." And if he once says
(10.224) that two heroes "go *together*" he does not form a
real compound and thinks more of the fact that their single
achievements are added together than that they are a real
unit.

In the *Odyssey* we find the word *synérithos* (6. 32): "a man
who works with someone else," "collaborator," "helpmate."
Athena appears to Nausicaa in a dream in the shape of one of
her close friends and offers to be a helpmate in washing the
clothes. But since this usage is unique, perhaps the word was
originally constructed like the later word *sýndoulos,* which
means "fellow slave," so that it was something like "fellow
workman."

Be this as it may. Even a word that later became very common—*sýmmachos,* "comrade in fighting," "ally"—is not to be
found in Homer but turns up for the first time in Archilochus
(frag. 75) and in Sappho. This shows that common actions,
common interests, common feelings had not yet come to the
attention of Homeric men as something remarkable and
specific. The appearance of these compounds with *syn* will
later help us to define where an action, a pattern of behavior,
or a feeling is regarded as something that is common to
various people.

Only if in a man's own mind he can feel united with someone else is it possible for him mentally to part with another
person. Only then can he feel isolated from those to whom he
belongs, alien to his neighbor, and lonely. On the other hand,
only if he can feel himself mentally connected with somebody

else is it possible for him to be divided in his own mind. An inner conflict or division within his mind indicates that he feels half of him belongs to one faction while the other half belongs to another.

Homer does not yet comprehend inner loneliness or inner discord. Let us consider inner conflict. It happens in Homer that someone "has two opinions," *diándicha mermerizei,* that he considers two possible aims for his action. But this is not yet a true inner conflict, for in the situations in which this phrase occurs the man does not have half his heart on one side of the question and the other half on the opposite side. There is absolutely no doubt in the man's mind as to what is useful or advantageous. The egoism of the Homeric heroes has been mentioned heretofore, and that there is a higher, more chivalric egoism which is concerned with man's honor. It is quite natural that conflicts may arise between a purely material profit and honor, or to take the extreme situation, between death and everlasting glory; there is no serious doubt that honor ranks higher than ordinary welfare, and uncertainty in a dilemma is concerned only with the means by which the better, the more advantageous issue can be achieved. The formula by which the solution of such a dilemma of "two opinions" is solved is: *doássato kérdion einai,* "it seemed more profitable," or *ariste phaineto boulé,* "it appeared as the best, as the most fruitful plan." Here the idea of advantage is definitely apparent. One can speak of a real cleavage or schism in the mind only if a man no longer knows absolutely what is good and what is evil. We shall return to this subject when tragedy is discussed.

The feeling of loneliness in the course of time became increasingly pronounced in Greek poetry; but Homer did not understand this feeling. Homer often says that somebody is alone or separated from others, *oios, moûnos, monōtheis, liastheis, apáneuthe*. But first of all this means only that he is separated from companions, for instance if he is cut off in battle from his friends (*moûnon eónta . . . apotméxantes . . . onì Tróessi monōtheis*) [8] Or it is said that a shepherd is alone in the field (*ē śe ge mounōthénta par' oúresin ē parà bousín*) .[9] If in three successive generations there has never been more than an only son, Homer can say: "So the son of Kronos has made our family lonesome" (*hôde gar hèmetérēn geneĕn moúnōse Kroniōn*) .[10] Laertes "no more comes to the town, but far off in the fields suffers misery" (*apáneuthen ep' agroû pĕmata páschei*) ; [11] but this misery is not so much a sorrow of the soul but a sorrowing over the wretched life he has to lead.

In none of these situations can the man who has been separated from others be regarded as lonesome in the sense that he feels a forlornness in his mind as the result of mental separation from those to whom he belongs.

Yet there are a few passages that are different. In the *Iliad* (1. 349) Homer says of Achilles in his anger: "But Achilleus weeping went and sat in sorrow apart from his companions beside the beach of the grey sea looking out on the infinite water."

Odysseus on the island of Kalypso longs for home: [12] "He was sitting disconsolate on the shore in his accustomed place, tormenting himself with tears and sighs and heartache, and looking out across the barren sea with streaming eyes." In a similar way Odysseus himself describes to Alcinoos how he

8. *Iliad*, 2. 467ff.
9. *Odyssey*, 15. 386.
10. *Odyssey*, 16. 117.
11. *Odyssey*, 1. 190.
12. *Odyssey*, 5. 82.

lived there (7. 258) : "But never for a moment did she win my heart. Seven years without a break I stayed, bedewing with my tears the imperishable clothes Calypso gave me." And most impressively Athena describes him (1. 49, 57) : "who has been parted so long from all his friends and is pining on a lonely island far away in the middle of the seas. . . . And Odysseus who would give anything for the mere sight of the smoke rising up from his own land, can only yearn for death."

Even these few places show some characteristic traits. The lonesome man who is separated from his friends (the *philoi* or *hetairoi*) weeps and complains; he sits on the shore and looks out over the sea. The separation is represented as a matter of fact, and he expresses his sorrow freely in laments and tears, of which the Homeric heroes generally do not yet feel ashamed. That feeling develops later when people believe that weeping discloses and betrays an inner mood. The pathos of the scene is especially impressive when the lonely man looks out over the desolate sea. Later on this becomes a typical landscape for loneliness. We shall find it again in Sappho and in Euripides. To us it is familiar through Goethe's *Iphigenia:*

> Und an dem Ufer steh ich lange Tage,
> Das Land der Griechen mit der Seele suchend.

> For days on end I stand upon the shore
> To seek the land of Greece with my own soul.

But there the "soul," as such, is explicitly designated.

3

EARLY ARCHAIC LYRIC POETRY

❖ ❖ ❖

VERY soon after Homer the Greek lyric poets considerably enlarged the possibilities of social groups that in the beginning had been so restricted, and quickly men learned to feel that they could be linked together in various new ways.

The earliest Greek lyric poet was Archilochus, who lived about 650 B.C. A man named Lykambes had promised to give him his daughter in marriage but afterwards failed to do so. In this failure to fulfill a promise Archilochus saw a breach of oath, and full of indignation he attacked Lykambes in a poem that relates the fable of the fox and the eagle. These two animals had founded a community (*xynōnie*) but the eagle destroyed the community by devouring the whelps of the fox. Revenge came about when the eagle took from an altar a piece of meat still glowing with fire, for upon taking it home he set fire to his nest and thus brought about the death of his own unfledged brood.

The same disappointment over a broken friendship is expressed by Archilochus in a poem recovered from a Strassburg papyrus (frag. 79 a) : he curses someone and wishes him stranded on the Thracian shore to become a slave of the barbarians. The poem ends with these words: "O could I see him there, who has done me such injustice, who has trampled down the oath,—and once he was my friend."

In both these poems—and we find similar ideas in other verses of his—he is linked to someone in a new personal and intensive manner, not only by convention, by family, by comradeship in arms, as we find the ties in Homer and Hesiod. Nor does Archilochus feel that his reputation or his honor has been injured—an insult that in Homeric times aroused men to anger and caused strife. Here a personal confidence that previously existed between the poet and another individual has been broken. Yet at the same time there had also existed an objective link—namely, justice. This justice is still seen in its religious implications: it is sanctioned by an oath, and Zeus, to whom the fox in the fable addresses his prayer, guarantees it. Therefore Archilochus reacts all the more violently when such a personal tie is ruptured.

All this becomes more apparent in Alcaeus, who lived about 600 B.C. (that is, fifty years later than Archilochus), and especially with the help of two poems recently found on papyri. Alcaeus was deeply involved in the struggles of political parties at Mytilene on the island of Lesbos. Together with Pittacus he had stood up against the tyrant Myrsilus. But later, when Pittacus gained power in Mytilene, Alcaeus regarded his former friend as a tyrant, a traitor, and an enemy.

Where now there was such a personal hostility, there had formerly been a very personal friendship: the two men had lived together in the same political convictions, had pursued

the same political aims of their party; thus they were united
by having the same friends and the same enemies. But that
does not mean they were of one *thymos,* of one mind in the
same way as Homeric heroes, for they did not find themselves
in the traditional situation of warriors fighting a common
foe.[1] Rather Alcaeus and Pittacus had stood together as two
individual men. As one poem explicitly states (frag. 129), an
oath founded the union of those who agreed mentally. It was
an oath resembling that described by Archilochus, and again
the erstwhile friend trampled upon the oath, as Alcaeus
explains with almost the same words used by Archilochus.

This poem says: Alcaeus stays in a large holy precinct, that
has been founded by the inhabitants of Lesbos, and that has
within it altars for Zeus, Hera, and Dionysus. Alcaeus lives in
wretchedness and in exile. Pittacus once belonged to the
hetairoi, the political friends of Alcaeus, and they had sworn
either to overthrow the tyrants and save the people from their
calamity, or to die together. But Pittacus has broken his oath
and now rages in the town like a beast of prey, without caring
for law and justice.

Hetairos here is not only a personal comrade, as in the
Strassburg poem of Archilochus, but a fellow member in a
political party. This is the first direct evidence of political
hetairiai, political clubs, as one usually calls them. This
conspiracy founded upon oaths can be dated in the nineties
of the sixth century B.C. Yet from later writers we know that
there had been such clubs before. For example, the attempt
of Kylon and his *"hetairia* of equals in age" to occupy the
Acropolis of Athens [2] and the overthrow of the rule of the

1. *Vide supra,* pp. 15-19.
2. Herodotus, 5, 71.

Penthelides by Megacles "and his friends" [3] date back to the
seventh century. It is quite possible that such *hetairiai* go
back to something very old, to primitive organizations in
which youths, upon reaching manhood, were initiated into
their tribes. But it is important to stress that now the cultic
and ceremonial union yields to a "political," and that means
to a new "mental," concord that apparently was not possible
before the seventh century.

The other newly found poem by Alcaeus was also written
while he was in exile (frag. 130). He expresses his feelings of
wretchedness for having to live in the rustic country, in the
eschatiai, as he describes it with a bit of exaggeration. In any
case, he is far from his friends, from all political activities
of market and council (*agorà* and *boulé*), and he has to live
all alone. He is uprooted out of the environment with which
he associates his true life—that is, the traditional social community of Mytilene.

But what is it that unites Alcaeus and his party? Is it some
idea, some program, or at least a common conviction? If the
fragment of a poem (67) that apparently mentions an oath
at the altar of Apollo is directed against Pittacus, then the
principal aim—and perhaps the only one—of taking the oath
was to see to it that none of the *kakopatridai*, who stemmed
from "inferior parents," should rise to power.

In any event, however, when Pittacus was at the helm, the
worst thing Alcaeus could say of him was that he had not been
born of noble parents. He varied this reproach in many ways
and often rudely. As far as we can tell, Alcaeus spoke only for
comrades who belonged together by virtue of their birth. But
apparently within his class of aristocrats there were different
groups who had loosely allied themselves together in factions,

3. Aristotle *Politics*, 1311 b 27.

each one of which possibly claimed to represent the genuine old nobility. It was a time when the ancient aristocracy was disintegrating and when through the development of industry and trade new classes achieved wealth and power. Hence the friends of Alcaeus were not yet held together by very much of a spiritual tie or by a well-defined theoretical program. But if a friend became an enemy and broke his oaths, the moral indignation on the part of Alcaeus was no less than it had been with Archilochus. "May the son of Zeus and grandson of Cronus look (upon me?)" was the beginning of a song in which he implored Apollo to wreak vengeance on Pittacus for breaking his sworn oath.

Though Alcaeus speaks surprisingly little about the ideas which really link him to his friends, his poems nevertheless (much more than those of Archilochus) reveal an awareness of being joined together with his friends—not only with single individuals but with a circle. Those bonds are evident in the compounds with *sym,* which appear for the first time in his poetry: "to come together," "to be together," "to be young together," and especially "to drink together," as well as the nouns derived from this verb: *sympotes* (the boon companion) and *symposium.* For Alcaeus drinking always means drinking together with friends. But of course Alcaeus and his friends do not meet regularly at their fixed club hours. They drink—or at least Alcaeus writes a poem for the party—only when there is a special occasion. The reason for celebration is in one instance unexpected joy over the death of the tyrant Myrsilus, in another happiness over the arrival of spring.

But in most instances it is distress or discomfort that drives Alcaeus to drink: the inclement weather, severe cold or cruel heat, intense fear of old age, death, or some other sorrow.

In any case, he does not offer us a trite merrymaking, as we find from the times of Anacreon and the pseudo-Anacreontic songs down to the student songs that can be bawled again and again every Saturday night. If he raises his voice, an actual agony of the moment stands before him, a menace to human existence; and his ability to grasp such harsh realities in his verses is greater than that of any other poet. It was obviously this ability that Horace especially admired in him. But Alcaeus scarcely endeavors to cope mentally with such anxieties. Wine is for him the expeller of care. He flees from reality into an oblivion of intoxication. Archilochus tried again and again to understand the alternation of good and evil; indeed he recognized a kind of law in these vicissitudes and learned to endure them. Nothing like that is found in Alcaeus.

Even in thinking through the motives for his political actions, though they preoccupy him strongly, he does not exert any individual initiative. Furthermore, he provides no really new meaning for the old notions of *hetairia,* oath, revenge of the gods, and aristocratic pride. In such reinterpretations others, above all Solon, will lead us ahead. The social and economic conflicts that existed in this time and that must have been important for the development of tyranny in Lesbos are not touched upon a single time by Alcaeus in the verses of his that have come down to us. It looks as though only certain noble families engage in the struggle for power. We see that individuals are somewhat freer to stand on one side or another, but the ideas and interests at stake in these struggles remain obscure.

Yet we would not do justice to Alcaeus if we did not stress one other point. It is from him that the Latin proverb *in vino veritas,* in wine there is truth (frag. 366), comes. Another proverbial saying of Alcaeus is: "Wine is the mirror of man."

Though he seeks oblivion in drink, nevertheless drunkenness brings forth truth—not, to be sure, truth that could explain the needs of our existence or could teach us how to manage them. The truth he means is that wine unveils the real mind of companions in the *symposium*: it reveals who is the genuine and trustworthy friend. In Attic drinking songs, in Theognis, and wherever political *hetairoi* meet at their usual tables, it is of vital importance to be able to rely upon the friend. A man would like to look into the friend's heart and put it to the test, as the analogy is often expressed, just as gold is tested by means of the touchstone.

At the moment when people join together because of the same intentions and notions, an accompanying feature is that a new dimension of the intellect is opened: the "true" meaning is to be discovered, the "depth" of the heart to be revealed. The difference between appearance and reality is strikingly emphasized for the first time in this difference between uttered words and hidden truth. This is not merely the distinction between a lie and a true statement, which was of course known to Homer too, because it does not concern an isolated utterance but the trustworthiness of the friend's state of mind. Nor is it the same as the artful deception of an enemy or of an unknown person who might be an enemy, as we find for instance with Odysseus, nor even the same as the betrayal of a friend, as described by Archilochus. Here we lack the well-defined situation in which someone either is a friend or is not a friend. Instead someone is a fickle friend who may one day turn out to be an enemy.

Though we do not learn this from Alcaeus, there can be little doubt that in Lesbos men were already beginning to grapple with intricate political conditions. This fact is revealed through Pittacus, who was entrusted with the reconciliation of opposing factions. In other Greek cities, similar attempts were made at that time. Pittacus was later counted among the Seven Sages, and several of these men seem to have impressed both contemporaries and successors with their attempt to overcome traditional views by means of their own mental initiative. Obviously it was no longer possible to bring under control the new social and economic situation with the conventional methods and institutions. The shift of wealth, which we observe at this time, was brought about by the fact that human invention and ingenuity had revolutionized the customary forms of agriculture, of crafts and arts, of trade and navigation. The improved plow made possible the cultivation of heavy soil and broke fresh ground for colonization; Pheidon of Argos invented coins which furthered the exchange of goods; in pottery, sculpture, and painting works of a previously unheard of excellence were produced. This progress spurred new demands upon politics to keep order or to restore it.

It is difficult, however, to determine in which particular details these "Sages" accomplished their tasks. Periander of Corinth, Bias of Priene, Chilon of Sparta remain mere shadows. Only one of them expresses himself to us convincingly through his verses, and obviously he is the greatest of all— Solon of Athens. But before we look at him more closely, I should like to speak of another poet who is somewhat earlier —Tyrtaeus, who, in the second half of the seventh century, admonished the Spartans with his elegies to be brave as they stood in difficult combat against the Messenians.

In his battle songs Tyrtaeus takes over much from the *Iliad* but expands it in such a manner that its significance extends beyond Sparta. His exhortations to the warriors differ from those of Homer in that for him, first of all, courage is the one and only estimable virtue. As early as the *Iliad* we find a specific use of the word "man" which implies that the real man is the brave warrior. With this idea in mind, Agamemnon (5. 529) or Ajax (15. 561) calls out: "Friends, now be men!" Homer has a word for "manhood" which means manly courage: *ēnorée*. This meaning of "man" moulds for Tyrtaeus the concept of a human being. He definitely refuses to recognize other virtues, capacities, or qualities, such as beauty, strength, wealth, eloquence. All those attributes are valueless compared to bravery. He does not, as far as we can see, use the word *ēnorée,* and he is not yet acquainted with the later word *andreia* ("manhood") for courage and *andreiós* ("manly") for brave. That usage is not exemplified before the fifth century; but for Tyrtaeus even more than for Homer there is only one "valor."

Another point in which Tyrtaeus in his exhortations differs from Homer is that the warrior must, as the poet repeatedly stresses, participate in the fighting with his "inner spirit": "Let us fight for our country with *thymos*" (6. 13): "One must stay in the forefront and stake one's *psyche* [life] and one's enduring *thymos*" (9. 18) ; and most clearly: "Make the *thymos* in your diaphragm great and stout" (6. 17) . This challenge, to transform the *thymos* in the interior of a man's body, is directed not only to single individuals but to all the Spartan youth, and they are exhorted to stand together spiritually. He does not spare heart-rending images to stir up the passions of the warriors: he who has to leave his home after a lost war roams about begging in a foreign country with his dear mother, his aged father, his small children, and his beloved wife (6. 4ff.) . It is a shameful sight if, in front of young warriors in the battle line, a hoary-headed old man lies slain in the dust, with his blood-stained genitals in his hands. Such

passages by far surpass anything that Homer says in order to
grip the soul.

You recall that Homer in some passages depicts the way in
which the Greeks stand close together in battle, having one
thymos. What Homer gives as a description becomes a command with Tyrtaeus: "Remain together" (6. 15), "don't
leave one another" (6. 20), "everyone must stand firmly in
his place" (8. 21). At this time the phalanx had just been
fully developed by the Greeks, and every single hoplite had
to participate not only for his own sake but also for that of
his neighbors. Unless everyone kept rank and with his shield
helped to protect at least the open flank of his left neighbor,
the phalanx would lose its striking power. This order that
had been carefully thought out made the Greeks superior to
other nations. Here too something common to the minds of
different men, the sense of responsibility, the obeying of
duty, or whatever we may term it, created a new kind of living together, and Tyrtaeus had good reason to call it to the
attention of the warriors.

But Tyrtaeus is concerned not only with the phalanx, this
highly successful implement of Spartan military tactics. He
says, after a long preamble (9. 15), in which he brings out
the virtue of the warrior in full relief: "It is a common good
[*xynón agathón*] both for the city and all her people, when a
man stands firm in the fore-front without ceasing." For Tyrtaeus there is such a thing as a "common good" for *polis* and
demos. Here for the first time something like a consciousness
of state appears. Homer had previously mentioned a "common evil" in the simile of the wasps in the sixteenth book of
the *Iliad* (v.262): If the silly boys tease the wasps nesting by
the wayside, they cause "a common evil for many," and in a
similar way, we might add, though the simile is not extended

that far, so did the Myrmidons who like wasps streamed from the ships. But here the word "common" does not have the strict denotation that makes us think of a community or a commonwealth. It means "general," "concerning many," without uniting these many into a solid group. Slightly different is its use in Archilochus, who says (frag. 51) : "For private profit they produced common evil;" here for the first time the opposition of personal and public welfare is formulated. But Tyrtaeus speaks of the common good in conjunction with *polis* and *demos,* with town and people, and means the state, to which everyone must subordinate himself.

This conception of the state originates with Tyrtaeus out of the situation created by war. The situation is entirely different a little later in the Athens of Solon, who achieves something even more essential and important for the future by working out his ideas about the state. Much more consciously than Tyrtaeus, much more radically and profoundly, he establishes in his verses the conception of the state on a spiritual basis, on the principle of justice.

Solon is forced to step in, not by problems of foreign politics but rather by domestic calamities that threaten to lead to civil war. It is a situation similar to the one in Lesbos, which we know from the verses of Alcaeus: the new economic conditions break up the old order, and new groups, upon gaining wealth, push their way to power.

But Solon does not simply join one of the existing groups, as Alcaeus did, and does not leave the ultimate victory merely to strength. Nor does he, as Tyrtaeus did, claim that one single quality or one virtue is virtue itself. He goes his own way.

In the *Elegy to the Muses* (1. 43ff.) he gives a broad picture of all the different activities and occupations of man without playing them off one against the other. Here for the first time a life of the citizenry appears and embraces numerous ways of life. Solon regards this multitude in two different aspects: the divine and the human. Some men have learned their crafts from Athena and Hephaestus; here he is thinking principally of the potters' and the smiths' arts—that is, of the industries coming into bloom at that time in Attica. Another sort, the poet, has been taught by the Muses; still another has been made a seer by Apollo. Others, such as surgeons, pursue the art of Paean. Solon sees only the human side of the merchant-sailor, who strives for profit, and the farmer, who toils the whole year long. But one thing is common to all—namely, that the end and success of their drudgery do not lie within their own hands. They strive and hope; they take the risk (*kindynos,* v.65) ; yet God alone decides the outcome. Thus a multitude of virtues is at the same time an abundance of deficiencies. Recognizing their value implies seeing their weaknesses too.

In this uncertain life one thing is certain: that justice will prevail. Whoever has acquired wealth by wickedness will receive punishment (1. 8ff.) ; Zeus surveys the end (1. 17) and sees to it that injustice is atoned for, even though it may be through the children and the children's children (1. 32). Dike, the goddess of justice, is a kind of Mnemosyne, who knows "what is and what has been"; she knows it "in silence," but in time will come to avenge (7. 15ff.) . In many single points Solon takes up what Hesiod developed out of Homer's conceptions of right, but he is the first to incorporate them in a political order.

That is how Solon constituted the beginnings of Athenian democracy. And if we today live together as we do or at least if we know fairly well how we ought to live together, then we owe our gratitude to him. Solon does not proceed from a theory of justice that he seeks to realize in practical life, but his exhortations aim, exactly as those of Tyrtaeus, at first of all removing an actual distress. Justice is above all the abolition of injustice; it curtails those who without any restrictions aspire to wealth and power.

If Solon steps in between the struggling parties and pushes into the focal point the question of justice, these tendencies are in accord with what also appears as new in other places at this time because a spiritual independence becomes apparent and because mental ties now hold society together. What happens here for the first time repeats itself again and again in the further development of the world. Men pledge themselves not to accept inherited conditions as static and valid facts but instead to try to improve them according to their own thinking. The mind thus projects a new political and social order.

Solon was able to counterpoise opposites because he himself had a well-balanced mind. When it was possible for him to become a tyrant himself, some reproached him, as he admits (23. 4), for having failed himself in *"thymos"* and "diaphragm," or as we would say: in resolution and in brains. He knew of course that he had both. But courage and intelligence are in a kind of dialectical tension with one another, and that is also true for the time before Aristotle dwelled upon the subject. In the epics called the *Aethiopis,* which were ascribed to Homer, this conflict was brought to a head in the following way: After the death of Achilles, his arms were to be handed over to the hero who was second in virtue. Hence the intelligent Odysseus and the brave Ajax competed for them. Because they were given to Odysseus, the decision was made in favor of intelligence. The quarrel about this continued even later. Pindar, for example, was very angry about this decision, and Aeschylus took it up again in a drama called *Hoplon Krisis*—that is, "The Decision Concerning the Weapons." Many of the arguments brought forward in this dispute were later taken over by Euripides in his *Antiope,* in which the value of practical and theoretical life is discussed.

It was particularly fortunate that Solon, this well-balanced man, acquired power and that his fellow citizens entrusted to him the reorganization of the state. It was good fortune, but even more what his merit deserved. He was able to manage affairs not by starting from one of the parties but from the very top. Thus there is nothing in his programmatic verses about the pathos of the suppressed that so often at the origin of modern democracies has injected a tone of hatred into political discussions. He could carry through his reforms soberly, objectively, trusting in divine order and justice, without struggling against a ruling class, for the wicked money-makers apparently belonged in part to the nobility and in part to the *nouveaux riches* of industry and trade. Furthermore, there was not yet at the time of Solon a question of anything like what in eighteenth-century Europe was called the *tiers état* or in the nineteenth century the proletariat. The slaves, the lowest stratum of the population, were taken into account only insofar as Solon freed those who had fallen into slavery through imprisonment for debt. That slaves too are men becomes clear to some enlighted souls, as we shall see, only about the end of the fifth century, and insurrections of slaves occur even much later.

Therefore, we must be careful not to see too much of modern humanitarian ideals in the reforms of Solon. Nor was he humanitarian in the sense that he thought man was principally good or that he attributed everything bad to the influ-

ence of social conditions, to an unfavorable milieu, and to
suppression. He did not hope that he could turn everything
to the better if he only improved the condition of those who
had come off badly. He did not start a revolution as a repre-
sentative of the poor, but, as a member of the old aristocracy,
he instituted reforms which took care of those who had been
reduced to poverty. What Solon fought was the preponder-
ance of private interests which opposed justice in the state.

When his fellow citizens subordinated themselves by their
own free will to the tyranny of Peisistratus, Solon commented
(frag. 8) : Each individual is foxy—that is, sly in looking after
his own benefit—but as a whole people are fools because they
have chosen slavery (*doulosýne*). "Slavery" here means the
condition of citizens under tyranny; the word "freedom" in
the sense of democratic freedom is not evident in Solon, but
since "slavery" is the life under a monarch (cf. 10. 3f.) and
in other passages the "free man" is contrasted with the slave
(24. 7 and 24. 13–15), there can be little doubt that Solon
was acquainted with the concept of political freedom as opposed to tyranny and that the idea in fact can be traced back
to him.

Reasonable and sane conditions are threatened by the
greed of individual persons, but the free state is founded on
righteousness, the power of which is guaranteed by Zeus.
Solon is liberal in acknowledging different ways of life, but
he does not compromise in postulating justice. In any case he
is not radical because right is for him not yet an abstract idea,
and therefore he does not attempt to inaugurate an ideal state
in this world. Right and Freedom are not as yet encumbered
with philosophical prerequisites, and that is the reason he is
free from the pathos of revolutionary idealism. Later enlight-
ened times are often inclined to sharpen the contrast between

friend and foe according to a political credo and to a standard of right and wrong fixed by the party in such a way that community life of the citizenry virtually disappears. On this point also, Solon is ready for compromise—he is democratic.

In his *Elegy to the Muses* (1.5) , Solon speaks about his relations with friends and enemies much in the old way of asking them to grant that he "be sweet to his friends, but bitter to his enemies, to the former a man deserving respect, to the latter a man terrible to behold." But after his reforms (cf. frag. 24. 18 and 24. 25) , he stresses that he has defended himself against encroachment from all sides and that he has permitted only Right to influence his actions. Only in this way has he been able to succeed in organizing the state upon a new spiritual principle. From his verses we can follow the way in which he formulates his program and, after having carried it out, defends it.

The poems of Solon make especially clear how economics, social problems, and political conditions are linked with the new interpretation of man, his mind, and his thought. The formation of factions within the state and the interweaving of common interests apparently precede reflections on the common ideas which keep a group together mentally. The process of growing self-interpretation of man and the discovery of the mind cannot possibly take place automatically in the airy sphere of pure speculation. As always, the mind here too is bound up with matter. But as I intimated just now, the economic and social conditions of the archaic period are dependent upon technical advances which again are effected through man's newly acquired awareness of his mental faculties and by a new confidence in them. Here it cannot be overlooked that the spiritual development proceeds in a certain direction and that the succession of different steps can, to a great extent, be followed up and understood, though the interplay of mind and body will always remain a mystery.

Wherever men unite mentally in this way, they separate themselves all the more sharply from others. If the parties within a state or the states themselves establish a program and base their unity on an ideology, they do not cease to have strife. On the contrary, struggles over mental issues usually are more violent than struggles for power. History shows that right up to our own day.

But let us turn to friendlier fields. During the same time that Alcaeus was living in Lesbos, Sappho was also flourishing there. With her the subjects we have been pursuing become even more apparent. She also finds herself bound to like-minded friends. Here too we find a group that grows beyond the old conventional bonds, and the essential thing is that the union is a mental one.

Sappho's circle feels united by a recollection of the beautiful things they have experienced together, and this memory lives on in poetry—for the Muses are the daughters of Mnemosyne. We find here just the opposite of what we saw in Alcaeus, who met his friends in the symposium in order to forget his sorrows by means of intoxication. Full of sadness she says (129) —obviously to a girl of her circle: "But you have forgotten me." Another time, in two papyrus fragments [4] she urges: "Remember, for we too have done this in the time of our youth; for many beautiful things. . . ." And as a friend takes leave of her in tears, she calls out to her (94.8) : "Remember me; for you know how we have cherished you. But if you don't remember, I shall remind you so that you won't forget how beautiful all our experiences were," and she enumerates all the joys they had together: the flowers

4. Joined by Mrs. E. M. Voigt, 24 (a) 2 and 29 (25) , in L.-P.

and precious unguents, the festivals in spring, the music. And
since her friend Arignota has returned to Sardes, she consoles
Atthis, who has remained behind, by saying that "Arignota
calls to mind the gentle Atthis, and in her tender heart is
weighted down with longing" (96). Remembrance, lovingly
preserved, overcomes spatial separation and, even more, the
distance of time. Thus memory takes over the old function of
Mnemosyne in a new form. Once the Muses, the daughters of
Mnemosyne, had kept alive the "imperishable fame" of the
hero in epics; now song, the gift of the Muses, accomplishes
what Thetis, when full of concern, had said to her son Achilles in the *Iliad:* "Tell me, that we both may know it."

Homer speaks of thoughts and of feelings only as far as they
give impulses to actions and happenings. Sappho begins to
dwell on moods and sentiments even if no activities originate
out of them. Sentiments become worthy of utterance since
they are an individual and significant state of the mind and,
above all, because men can join through them and can remain joined by remembrance, whose sole aim is to preserve
and keep alive what once has been felt.

One fragment of Sappho (55) gives a religious significance to this thought, and therefore perhaps is more important than one is inclined to suppose today. It is directed, as
the authors who quote it maintain, against an uneducated
rich woman or against one who lives without the Muses and
lacks knowledge.

The verses run as follows: "When you are dead, you will
lie unremembered for ever; for you have no part in the roses
that come from Pieria and you will be obscure in the house
of Death too, and you will roam about among the faint dead
after you have flitted away from here." Taking part in the
roses of the Muses are those who can appreciate poetry and

music; but excluded are those who, as the authors quoting these verses put it, are unlettered and "unmusical." Apparently Sappho speaks to someone who does not belong to her circle and who has no sense of its pleasures.

Certainly these verses do not maintain that Sappho expects a genuine afterlife of the soul for herself or her friends, but they do show that she gives those with whom she feels mentally united considerable reason to hope for an existence beyond death, even though it may be only that the friends whom she names live on with her in her songs. Thus these verses are our earliest evidence for the assertion that in a circle of like-minded people some eschatological hopes are entertained. Here the point is not that, as in the old epics, the name of an individual lives on because a song celebrates his deeds, but it survives because he has taken part in a life that was especially close to the gods, to the Muses in particular. "The house of the servants of the Muses is pure;" "Somebody, I tell you, will remember us hereafter," Sappho says in other passages.

This new intensity of living together creates a new feeling of loneliness. Homer had depicted the solitude of man as an objective fact, as separation from others, which he had occasionally made impressive by placing the lonely person beside the sea. Much more movingly, in a nocturnal scene apparently at the seashore, Sappho describes Arignota, who though she "shines among the women of Lydia as the moon among the stars, wanders to and fro, and with longing calls to mind the gentle Atthis." The sufferings of the soul as a result of separation and loneliness are expressed here much more strongly than ever before, and at the beginning of this fragment Sappho adds: "Arignota has her mind, her *noos*, here with us." More distinctly than in any other passage of the early period, this line of Sappho says that the mind can detach itself from the body and can exist in another place. This means of course that the mind or the soul is something truly incorporeal.

If Sappho feels that she is bound to the women of her circle by the common memory of beautiful things, then "beautiful" here means something different from what one generally associates with the term. In the sixteenth poem she very explicitly declares that for others a cavalry parade, hoplites, or a navy may be the most beautiful thing; but for her the most beautiful is "that which one loves." Remembering Anaktoria, she says she would rather see Anaktoria's gentle step and the bright gleam on her face than the Lydian chariots and the armored infantry.

This more intensive and more personal feeling for beauty is common to her circle, and together they keep the beautiful alive in their memory. But though this new love of beauty is different from what ordinary mortals may regard as beautiful, nevertheless it is a gift of the gods, of Aphrodite, as in this poem, or of Eros, the Muses, the Charites, as it is in other poems of Sappho. Thus a more personal relation to the divinity is established. Certainly Odysseus and Telemachus in the *Odyssey* are the favored friends of Athena, but Sappho and her beloved friends feel that they see something more in Aphrodite than other human beings who believe they are close to the goddess.

At the time of Sappho new religious cults were springing up in other parts of Greece. These sects fostered common ideas of a pure life on earth and common hopes for a life beyond death. They differed from traditional religious practice in that they developed special mysteries which, to be kept secret, had to be withheld from the uninitiated. That is why

we know so little about cults such as the Orphics, the Pythagoreans, the Eleusinians, and so forth. But the main point is
perfectly clear: they differed from primitive secret organizations, in which a group composed of the traditionally associated members of a society participated in occult rites—say
men or women, boys or girls, a certain caste or professional
group. In the new religious cults, admission to the group depended solely on a personal desire to participate in a common
belief and its common hopes.

Soon after this time philosophical schools were started, and
a great variety of other new groups began to thrive. All of
these groups were characterized by the fact that they were
founded and organized according to a definite plan and that
they were held together by common mental or spiritual interests.

4

LATE ARCHAIC LYRIC POETRY

❖ ❖ ❖

NEVER in European history has there been a time so rich in fundamentally new ideas as the epoch of early Greek lyrics. If at that period new economic possibilities, such as circulation of money and colonial expansion over wide areas of the Mediterranean coast, loosened the traditional forms of society, the family, the clan, and the tribe, they also gave birth simultaneously to new mental forces enabling man to build up new social groups. The poets resolutely led the way in this new development. A new feeling of personal and inner friendship appeared with Archilochus and Sappho, a new political solidarity among party members was felt by Alcaeus, and Tyrtaeus and Solon gave evidence of a new sense of responsibility toward the state.

All these poets are convinced—however different may be their concepts of what unites the like-minded—that the significant value of the unifying principle is immediately apparent. Sappho, for instance, says explicitly when she depicts her new and deeper conception of what is beautiful (16.6) : "It is easy to make this understandable to everyone." All these poets are unfalteringly serious in their concern and therefore muster all their emotion. What they regard as essential, though it be comprehended in a personal way, actually exists as something objective and something which stems from the gods.

Even Mimnermus, the most sceptical of early Greek poets, does not find life problematic. Man, though he may be transitory and frail, does not doubt what is worth striving for. Though pleasure may be evanescent, it nevertheless is still pleasure.

In the middle of the sixth century there is a large gap in poetry, and when at the end of the century important poets again speak to us, many things have changed. The reason that the thoughts of man about himself and about his attitude toward the world and his fellow men have shifted is shown by Simonides in his drinking song to the Thessalian Skopas (frag. 4), important parts of which have come down to us because Socrates discusses them at length in Plato's *Protagoras* (339 Aff.). The poem begins with the words: "It is difficult to be truly [*alāthéōs*] a good man [*anèr agathós*]." The "good" man, the "able" man we have previously encountered in Tyrtaeus. Of all the virtues and capacities of men he had appreciated only valor that proves itself in battle. Simonides does not aim, as Tyrtaeus did, or as in another way Solon did, at giving prominence to one single virtue as the true and genuine virtue among many others, but as subsequent parts of the poem will show, he has in mind the universal collective virtue that comprises all single virtues. He is not concerned with selecting from among the different values that have been recognized before, but rather with a thorough comprehension of the essential nature of virtue. He takes the word "good" seriously in a new sense. Similarly, other Greeks of these early times reflect upon the "true meaning" of a word, and this process at once leads to philosophy.

We have encountered this search for true meaning in two previous instances. Sappho, for example, thought "real" beauty is that which one loves even if it is simple and unpretentious, like the radiant smile on the face of a friend. Then too, Alcaeus said that wine is a mirror for disclosing the "real" friend. Both poets gave a diagnosis of something that was external to them but attached to them mentally. Simonides, however, intends something quite different. He takes up an expression of Pittacus: it is difficult to be noble. This need not mean more than that man is limited in his capacities and that, according to the assertion of Hesiod,[1] virtue is difficult to achieve and that the gods have set sweat before virtue (and success). But by setting up an opposition in which reality is balanced against outward appearance—that is, by using the categories Sappho and Alcaeus applied to the diagnosis of genuine beauty and of a genuine friend—he changes the meaning:

To become a truly good man is difficult, even if he is fashioned without flaw in hand, foot, and mind, four-square. . . . Such is the lot of a God alone; as for a man, he cannot but be evil if he be overtaken by hopeless calamity. For any man is good in good fortune and bad in bad, and take it in all, they are best who are loved by the Gods.

Out of all that Simonides draws this conclusion: "My praise and friendship is for all those who do nothing disgraceful voluntarily." This last word (hekōn) had since the days

1. Quoted by Simonides himself in his frag. 37, and drawn into the discussion by Socrates in Plato's *Protagoras*, 240 D.

of Hesiod [2] and of Solon become more and more important in jurisprudence in order to distinguish an intentional perjury or murder from an unintended injury. That is how the reflection upon what is really good becomes a speculation not only about certain friends but about human nature in general. And that, in fact, is the goal of Simonides from the very beginning.

In our context this is interesting only insofar as it affects life in human society. It has been taken for granted that a man wished to be good, and this was almost a matter of course as long as "good" was not a strictly moral notion but denoted "able" or "successful." Just as today every football player wants to be a good football player, so in those times every man wanted to be a good man. But when reflection starts to take the word seriously and teaches how to distinguish between what is truly good and what only seems to be so, then what is good begins to depart from this world and to become something unattainable. It approaches the realm of the divine, and the chasm between men and gods becomes all the larger. Man then exerts increasingly greater efforts to feel at ease and at home on this earth, which he had always known to be imperfect. But once imperfection is taken as a moral issue, once the actions and deeds of man prove to be paltry, then pleasure in this world is more thoroughly embittered. This is the malaise the poets had to cope with after the second half of the sixth century. Simonides in his *skolion* to Skopas tries to get around it with a mild resignation. This is characteristic of his own personality but is not to be found in any other poet of the time. Yet the greater tension between a world interpreted in an unsophisticated way and the higher

2. *Theogony*, 232.

claims of the "knowing" man is evident in all the poets of the late archaic age.

In Simonides a more refined feeling leads to the beginnings of sentimentality and a more conscious thinking leads to a cleverer wit. The earliest example—and a very beautiful one too—of incipient sentiment appears in Simonides' description of Danae, who is enclosed with her little son Perseus in a wooden box and drifts over the stormy sea (frag. 13.). Everything in the poem is tuned to pathetic contrasts: the roaring waves and the sleeping baby, the cruelty of nature and the tenderness of the mother, the wild despair and the resignation of Danae. At this point we will not pursue the subject of how these tender descriptions were amplified many times in the great choral lyrics. I mention only how Pindar depicts little Iamos in the sixth Olympian ode (v.53ff.) and how Bacchylides ends his sixteenth dithyramb with a passionate address to the unfortunate Deianira.

The beginning of wit is shown clearly in one of Simonides' victory songs and in what Aristotle tells us about it. A southern Italian tyrant had asked Simonides to praise a victory he had won with a team of mules. The poet refused because mules were not a worthy subject for poetical art. But when he was offered an increased honorarium, he undertook the poem, which he began with these words: "Hail, ye daughters of stormfooted steeds!" (frag. 19). The poet had to deal with a rich person who had commissioned a work of art. In early archaic times this particular situation did not exist. But as economic advancement blossomed all over Greece, a newly gained wealth wished to display itself in works of art and poetry; and especially the tyrants drew sculptors, painters, and poets to their courts. Thus it became a concern of the poet to

maintain his dignity of intellect in face of the patron's over-
whelming power.

Even more wittily Ibycus is successful in this somewhat pre-
carious situation. A papyrus has preserved large parts of his
poem in honor of Polycrates, the tyrant of Samos. He says
something like this: "Once the Greeks besieged Troy and
waged the war, so often celebrated in song, because of Helen's
beauty. Now I will not sing about Paris, who cheated his host,
nor about Cassandra and the other children of Priam or the
doom of Troy. Nor shall I dwell on the heroic deeds of the
Greeks who came in ships and whom Agamemnon led. The
wise Muses alone can record all the single facts about the fleet
that took the Achaeans from Aulis at that time. Amongst
them was the splendid Achilles and Telamon's son Ajax." In
the following verses that are badly damaged, the most handsome Greek is mentioned, but we cannot make out whom
Ibycus names as such. Then he refers to Troilus as the most
handsome Trojan and ends the poem with the words: "Together with these you also, Polycrates, will always have imperishable fame for beauty [here he uses the very old phrase
áphthiton klěos], as far as that depends upon my song and
upon my fame."

In such a song of praise it is customary to exalt the person
addressed with a myth. The myth of course can do this only
if the audience sees the relationship between the tale and the
person praised. If this relationship is not apparent, the myth
is without meaning. Now it becomes obvious that in narrat-
ing the expedition of the Greeks against Troy Ibycus especially emphasizes the great fleet of Agamemnon. "The wise
Muses alone can record all the individual details of the ships,
but not ordinary mortals," Ibycus says, and this is a quotation
from the invocation to the Muses at the beginning of the

ships' catalogue in the second book of the *Iliad*. To me, at any rate, it seems evident that if this poem is addressed to a Polycrates, he can be none other than the tyrant of Samos, who in fact achieved his mighty dominion by virtue of his fleet. Ibycus is not so gross as to hurl this flattering comparison into the king's face. "I shall not talk about this," he says —it goes without saying that you are powerful like Agamemnon because of your ships. But the other things too upon which Ibycus does not want to dwell are full of allusions. "I shall not praise Paris, who cheated his host"—we learn from Pindar that he interpreted his relationship to the person who commissioned the poem from him to be that of guest-friendship. Thus the poet gives the song to his host as the gift of an appreciative guest, and in return he receives a present—we dare not breathe the word "fee." Greek aristocratic society ignored modern conceptions of rational counting and monetary systems, and kept alive (at least in words) the ancient forms of economic exchange, reciprocal gifts, and countergifts. Therefore, it seems to me, Ibycus refuses with good reason to speak about a man who violated hospitality. "Nor shall I sing about Cassandra and the other children of Priam or the doom of Troy"—since it is a day of merry festival, gloomy thoughts must be kept far away.[3] The graceful turn at the end then means: "That you, Polycrates, are like the worthiest Greek heroes, I need not mention, and I shall not do it today, but I do mention that you are as handsome as the most handsome, and through that you will achieve fame." With this tribute Ibycus makes the song appropriate for a joyful symposium, in which it was not uncommon to praise the beauty of a friend.

But what makes the poem relevant in our context lies in

3. Cf. Stesichorus, frag. 12 and 22.

the last six words: *hōs kat' aoidàn kai emòn klĕos,* "as far as that depends on my song and on my fame." As the fame of the ancient heroes had become immortal only because Homer had sung it and his poems have outlasted his time, so too the fame of Polycrates is dependent on the song and on the fame of Ibycus.

This is courtly poetry. Though it is certainly blatant flattery, Ibycus does not compromise himself; for he says, playfully but clearly, that he is the equal of the tyrant. All this power and glory avail him nothing unless the poet preserves them for recollection—and he was right.

The poet thus achieves a new position in a changed society, and Ibycus seems to have done much to attain it for him. Now the poet is actually forced to break loose from the old conventions and to exert his own mental powers in order to live up to an entirely new situation. Of course the intellectual response of genuine poetry is more important for this "new art" than the relationship to a mighty person who commissions a poem. From the speculations of Simonides about the truly "good" man and from his tender description of Danae we see that it is not just the challenge of someone like a king that leads him to deeper feeling and thinking. Yet it cannot be denied that the poets of this time—including Pindar, Bacchylides, and Anacreon—are greatly influenced by their social background.

The greatest of these poets is Pindar, who brings forth the new ideas in the most original manner. Since he resists so many of the innovations arising in his time, one tends to regard him too exclusively as a defender of the old concept of nobility, of the Doric "virtue" (*aretĕ*), and of the aristocratic constitution. But where this seemingly conservative poet expresses himself fundamentally and programmatically about

his art—namely in some verses preserved on a partially damaged papyrus—he sounds quite different: [4] "Let the hymns
resound, but don't go in the beaten tracks of Homer, but
with new horses, since I have mounted the winged chariot of
the Muses. . . . [there is a gap here] but I pray to Mnemosyne and her daughters to give me the necessary ability. For
the mind of a man is blind, if he tries without the aid of the
Muses to explore the deep way in the wisdom of mortals (?).
But upon me [the Muses?] conferred this work. . . ."

It is worth while to compare these verses of Pindar with
those of Callimachus, the great Hellenistic poet who two
hundred years later uses them in the prologue of his *Aitia*.
Callimachus relates that during his first attempts to write
poetry Apollo told him: [5] "And then I command you to go
on tracks that are not used by carriages, not in common with
others nor on the large streets, but on the paths that no one
has touched, though they be narrow." Though Callimachus
borrows from Pindar almost literally, he means something
quite different. His intention is to defend his new Hellenistic
theory of art, art for art's own sake, which addresses itself to
a fastidious, sophisticated public. He seeks not only "new"
paths, but "narrow" ones; he avoids the broad highways.
Since he wants to create small delicate shapes, he does not
speak of a "winged chariot of the Muses," as Pindar does; he
rather despises everything sublime.

Pindar's own concern becomes apparent when we try to
consider, though we can do that here only in a superficial
survey, where the subject matter of this fragmentary paean
turns up in other passages of Pindar and his contemporaries.
To begin with form: Pindar employs new meters. Whereas

4. *Paean*, VII b 5ff.
5. Frag. 1. 25 Pfeiffer (Callimachus, vol. 1, Oxford 1949).

the lyric poets of early archaic times had constructed their songs out of single rhythmical divisions or periods that were rigidly fixed, Pindar breaks down these old traditional forms and introduces a free personal movement into the rhythms. This is an especially clear symptom of his deliberate effort to change the tradition. He also tries to reform the established kinds of ritualistic songs. At least one example shows how he converts the old structure of a sacred choral hymn: in the second dithyramb he makes fun of how "once the song of the dithyrambs was long drawn out," but now a "new" kind prevails. This sounds almost like a programmatic statement, though it does not signify what is later meant by Callimachus, who is much more radical in his endeavor to create new forms of art. Pindar, however, keeps the pith of the old songs and only tries to reform and refashion them.

Other poets at this time go even further than Pindar in dissolving the ancient forms of poetry, though Pindar seems to have been the most determined reformer of metrics. In any case, others do not refrain from giving new meanings to old genres of poetry. Timocreon of Rhodes, for example,[6] uses the form of an encomium for an invective against Themistocles (frag. 1) ; whereupon someone [6] abuses Timocreon in the form of an epitaph (frag. 99) and in this way creates the satirical epigram, which later has such an extensive development. Bacchylides too, in his poem on Marpessa (frag. 20), seems to have used the encomium to rebuke someone, apparently the father of a girl, although the usual form for a vituperative poem since the time of Archilochus had been the epode or the iambus.

Even in the forms of choral hymns, which had been fixed by definite rites, the boundaries between different genres begin to blur. That is shown by the fragments of a commentary

6. It was later thought to have been Simonides.

on Bacchylides' *Cassandra* (c.23) recently published in the *Oxyrhynchus Papyri* (23. 2326): Callimachus thought this poem was a paean or song to Apollo because the customary invocation (*ié*) occurred in it. Aristarchus, on the other hand, thought it rather a dithyramb because the story of Cassandra was related in it. "Aristarchus gave it the title Cassandra," the commentator continues and obviously presupposes that dithyrambs at this time ought to bear titles. This assertion is explained by the fact that at festivals for Dionysus, as we know was the case in Athens, there were literary competitions for dithyrambs similar to those held for tragedies. But since the stories which make up the Dionysus myth did not suffice for all the choral songs year after year, poets had to look for other legendary material. And, in fact, we find that the dithyrambs of Bacchylides treat very different myths. These poems received titles, just as the tragedies did, because it was necessary to distinguish from one another the songs entered in competition for the prize.

The confusion is even greater in the case of two poems found on a papyrus, both of which are probably by Bacchylides (frag. 60 and 61). The first ends with the invocation to Apollo: *ié ié;* the second has as its title "The Leucippides" but then begins telling us that girls establish a "newly resounding choir of fair aspect for the violet-eyed Aphrodite." Here too we probably have a dithyramb that has freed itself from the old ritual scheme and has become "literature."

Of course the old forms of dithyrambs continued to exist. Pindar, for instance, seems to have produced one on the market place of Athens as a genuine ritual song for the festival held at the Altar of the Twelve Gods, as K. F. Johansen recently showed.[7] On the other hand, the fact that Pindar also begins to treat the traditional forms as mere literary frame-

7. *Kongelige Danske Videnskaberner Selskab*, 4, 2, 1959, 37.

work is shown by the third Pythian ode, which (unlike his other extant songs of victory) was not composed to be performed at a specific festival but was sent to Hieron in Syracuse as a letter of consolation.

Though the old forms begin to disintegrate, the late archaic choral lyrics essentially maintain the old genres and their religious function. Yet the poets have a lively awareness that they want to provide something new and that they are able to do so. I prefer not to cite an accumulation of passages to prove this now but to mention only a few that characterize more precisely this consciousness of their own original contributions. A few selections will show that they mean more than Phemios, who says in the *Odyssey* (22. 347) that god has implanted to his mind various paths of song and thinks of the many stories he can tell.[8]

Pindar says:[9] "Thanks to the gods, I have countless paths opening on every side," and Bacchylides (19. 1; cf. 5. 31), using almost the same words: "There are countless paths of immortal songs for him that is dowered of the Pierian Muses." Both of these poets, regardless of who may have uttered this thought first, feel capable of new achievements because many possibilities are open to them. They do not merely feel the greater mobility of their own minds—and to be able to play with different possibilities is, in fact, an indication of a freer mind. But Pindar adds: "Thanks to the gods," and Bacchylides: "Who is dowered of the Muses."

This sounds as though both have remained in the old piety and regard their achievement as a grace and gift of the gods. But it cannot be overlooked that their relationship to the gods differs from that of Archilochus or Sappho. Archilochus

8. Cf. 1. 352; Alcman, frag. 7; Stesich., frag. 25.
9. *Isthmian*, 3. 19.

(frag. 1) called himself a servant of Ares and someone skilled in the gift of the Muses. Sappho (frag. 150) spoke about the house belonging to servants of the Muses, meaning her own house and that of her friends. Pindar and Bacchylides grasp for larger words when they explain their relationship to the Muses.

Pindar calls himself "the tuneful prophet of the Muses." [10] He addresses the Muses (frag. 150) : "Give the oracle, I shall proclaim it as prophet." And when he seems to speak of his own poetic abilities, he says: [11] "Like a prophet-priest I shall accomplish it." Bacchylides even calls himself "the divine prophet of the Muses" (9. 3).

Both are no longer content to be simple servants, but by stressing their solemn mission they emphasize the spiritual dignity to which they aspire as poets. Up to this time no poet had spoken of himself in such a lofty strain. We have seen how Ibycus had found a way to stress the worth of his poetry and to appear as an equal of a mighty tyrant of this world, whose deeds could survive only if the poet immortalized them. Out of these ideas Pindar creates a kind of philosophy: all things in this life are so interwoven that they are dependent on one another, and in this condition a mutual "need" or "want" (*chrĕos*) exists between great virtue and wise poetry. Here the old opposition of virtue (*aretĕ*) and wisdom (*sophía*) comes up again. We have seen that in early times virtue mainly consisted in valor but that in the conflict between Ajax and Odysseus about the weapons of Achilles the *sophía* of Odysseus had challenged the old ideal of "manhood" represented by Ajax. In Pindar we find that the two sides have moved farther apart and that there is a beginning

10. *Paean*, 6. 6.
11. *Parthenia*, 1. 5.

of the later distinction between *vita activa* and *vita contemplativa*. We shall have to return to this when we speak of Euripides.

The new sublimity of poetry which we encounter especially in Pindar is important as a reflection of social conditions. It shows that now a poet can count on a public that accepts his exalted pretensions and is capable of appreciating such thoughts, even though (as the poet admits) these thoughts go beyond the horizon of ordinary people.

When Pindar makes known what a deeper insight has revealed to him, he does not address just the single person for whom he created the poem. Nor does he write for merely a small group of intimate friends like that to which Sappho explained the nature of beauty, or a group of *hetairoi* such as Alcaeus addressed. Pindar, to be sure, speaks to a larger audience, especially in his hymns to the gods that were performed at public festivals. Certainly Tyrtaeus and Solon had addressed their elegies to all the citizens, but their aim was immediate political exhortation, and that kind of propaganda was no longer of any concern to poets of the late archaic period. Pindar and Bacchylides continue the tradition of the Homeric bards—a tradition which had been introduced into choral lyrics by Stesichorus about the time of Sappho—and in fact they often perform before the same public that listens to recitations of Homeric epics. While the community at large still appreciates the old tales of heroic adventures, it is open-minded enough to lend an ear to new poetical aspirations and rather sophisticated poetry in a way that was previously unheard of. This shows that the social background of these choral lyrics is something more than the relation between the poet and a mighty tyrant.

In our context it is not so important that Pindar and Bacchylides interpret their poetical *sophia* or "wisdom" in quite different ways. Bacchylides (frag. 5) says: "Now as of yore one acquires skill from another to find the gates of words unsaid before." A new poem, he thinks, arises at any given time when a poet advances and improves upon the materials already existing. On the other hand, Pindar believes: [12] "The wise poet is he who knows many things by gift of nature [*phyâi*]; but they that have only learnt are turbulent and intemperate of tongue like crows." This is, as the early commentators observe with apparent accuracy, a gibe at Simonides and Bacchylides. Pindar regards himself as an aristocrat who was born with all that anyone could desire, whereas Bacchylides knows he is living in a constantly developing tradition since he has always learned from others.

But though Bacchylides gives much more credit to the achievements of his predecessors, he surpasses even what Pindar says about his prophetic mission. He calls himself not just a prophet but, as we have seen, a divine prophet. One can imagine that this must have jarred somewhat on the nerves of Pindar, who therefore styles his fellow poet a crow.

More important differences between the two become apparent if we ask what each of them looked upon as the content of his wisdom. As far as we can see, Bacchylides is not explicit, but he continues what we found with his uncle Simonides—that is, not so much his wit as a tendency to bring out in relief the pathetic and moving elements in a myth. He does this often to the extent of omitting actual well-known facts and concentrating on the feature most essential to him—the sentiment.

Pindar, on the other hand, again and again reflects upon his art—what it really is and how he can give evidence of it.

12. *Olympian*, 2. 82.

He is not content with Simonides' wit and sentiment. He calls his art "wisdom," *sophía,* but not in the old sense of the word, which could be applied to a wise poet, a wise surgeon, or a wise charioteer. In these instances "wise" means that someone is well versed in his craft. But Pindar's wisdom aims at truth—truth so linked up with virtue, *areté,* the praise of which is his task, that he can call it the beginning of virtue (frag. 205): "You, beginning of great virtue, O Queen Truth, keep me from stumbling against rough falsehood." This one sentence is enough to show that Pindar, when he cautions against following in the beaten tracks of Homer, does not, like Callimachus, want to propagate a new aesthetic theory that concentrates on the technical mastery of his art. In the previously mentioned paean, in which Callimachus found the words about new approaches to poetry, Pindar continues: "Blind is the mind of the man who, without the Muses, tries to explore the deep way in the wisdom of mortals."

He aims at something objective, something capable of being known—that is, cognition. But this truth, which blind mortals do not see, has not simply come to him, as the tale of the Muses occurs to the Homeric bard. In the fragment of this paean Pindar says that truth is something one "tracks" or "noses out" (*ereunâi*), and immediately after that he speaks of his song as a "labor," a *ponos.* Here for the first time the idea is expressed that a man can and must toil in his mind, and especially important is the image of "tracking." Homer uses this verb for a lion or for hounds that seek a trail, and later this hunting image occurs frequently in Plato. Since Socrates, man has realized that he cannot grasp the whole truth but can only track it and explore it. This conception becomes possible only when one no longer sees the mind as an organ being affected from the outside but as something incorporeal acting out of its own impulse. On the way to a more "abstract" conception, this verse of Pindar is an important landmark.

Once we have noticed this, we shall see that Pindar very often is on a quest and that he "finds" his poems.[13] "The Muse has stood beside me when I found out a tune bright and new."[14] "Let us find a friendly song in honor of Aetna's king."[15] "Many a tale has been told in many a way. But for anyone to find new things and submit them to the touchstone for assay, is perilous indeed."[16] We have met this testing on the touchstone as a means of proving a true friend. Pindar also uses the image in such a context,[17] but for him it belongs to a larger field of seeking out genuine truth: "We [that is, the poets] teach that something is gold with the help of the pure touchstone" (frag. 122. 16). But he knows that man is limited in this endeavor: "He can't track the plans of the gods with his human mind, for it descends from a mortal mother" (frag. 61).

In everything that has come down to us by tradition, Pindar apparently stresses the importance of investigating the truth, with the help of witnesses, with the aid of proof, and above all—and here some difficulties arise—with the consciousness that only what is beautiful and bright can really be true. "The immortals apportion to man two trials for every boon they grant. This foolish men cannot bear with a good grace, but the noble can, by ever turning the fairer side

13. Cf. Alcman, frag. 92; Stesich., frag. 14.2.
14. *Olympian,* 3. 4.
15. *Pythian,* 1. 60.
16. *Nemean,* 8. 20.
17. *Pythian,* 10. 67.

to the front." [18] All Pindar's poetry is directed so exclusively toward praise—to glorify a god or to glorify a man—that the very ground would be removed from under his feet if the world were not praiseworthy. But if, as he says, twice as much suffering as good fortune befalls man, the good and noble man will turn what is beautiful to the outside, just as he would turn the better portions of a worn garment. This contrast between the gloomy experiences of life and a belief in the order and beauty of the world repeatedly occupies Pindar's thoughts.

Above all, Pindar is in search of truth in myths. For him the gods and heroes have become so sublime that he can no longer believe they might have done anything objectionable. Yet myths are full of scandal. But since Pindar cannot accept the offensive portions as true, he either suppresses them or, if necessary, gives them a new interpretation. In *Nemean*, 5. 13ff., when he ought to mention that the heroes of Aegina, Peleus and Telamon, have slain their stepbrother Phocus, Pindar says: "Reverence restrains me from telling of a mighty deed,—haply hazarded in no righteous wise. . . . I will halt: it is not every truth that is the better for showing its face undisguised; and full oft is silence the wisest thing for a man to devise."

Here the traditional attitude—or call it the aristocratic, the noble, the high-minded attitude—shows itself to be stronger than his quest of truth. Pindar indeed is no more radical about truth than he is about morality. For instance, he is not so unconventional as either Xenophanes, who condemns the gods for not living according to bourgeois morality, or the tragedians, who pose the question of justice in a more serious, fundamental, and radical way.

18. *Pythian*, 3. 83.

So with Pindar the myths are in a curious state of suspension. They do not remain the old sagas that certainly depicted a life which, though higher, was still one to which all passions and even gloom and cruelty were familiar. For Pindar myths belong to a purer and more beautiful world; in fact, they acquire some utopian traits. And no one has painted this bright mythical world so enchantingly as Pindar.

The difficulties Pindar encounters when trying to show that this divine realm is not only fair but also real become apparent in two passages explaining the criteria for determining the truth of a traditional story. In *Olympian,* 1. 35 he says: "The days that are still to come are the wisest witnesses;" and in *Olympian,* 10. 54: "*Chronos* [Time] is the only one who by examining brings to light the real truth." Especially the first sentence seems to have been formulated by him in an intentionally paradoxical form; for, properly speaking, the most reliable witness is the man who was present, who was nearest to the event. But for Pindar truth results from searching and tracking and can appear only in the course of time. But then truth is something different from what the lawyer or the scientist (who after Kant also becomes an examiner of witnesses) can recognize.

Though Pindar ascribes his achievements to the grace of the gods, he is not hesitant about awarding himself a "great mind" (*noos*) : "One is the race of men, one is the race of gods, and from one mother do we both derive one breath; yet a power that is wholly sundered parts us, in that the one is naught, while for the other the brazen heaven endures as an abode unshaken for evermore. Albeit, we mortals have some likeness, either in great mind or in nature, to the immortals." [19] The idea that a "great mind" can distinguish a

19. *Nemean,* 6. 1ff.

person appears here for the first time, and when Pindar says that such a great mind draws a man nearer the gods, we remember that he regards himself as a seer or a prophet. But of course he does not articulate clearly in this passage wherein he claims a great *noos* for himself.

This is not the place to show in detail how Pindar proves his great mind above all by demonstrating the connections and harmonies of the world, by exploring again and again how mortals and immortals, the present and the myth, the great deed and the song are mutually interrelated, by making "long leaps" occasionally [20] to connect things that seem to be separated, and by reproducing in his verses all the bright things that receive their splendor from one divine light.

If the poet needs a "great mind" to do justice to everything great, beautiful, and true that he explores and praises, then he interprets "mind" as something more abstract than his predecessors did, since it is more "active" and more "cohesive."

No one in history has attributed to poetry an importance such as Pindar has given it. For him poetry gives the world its ultimate perfection. When Zeus instituted the order of the cosmos and when the Olympian gods came into being, he asked them (frag. 31) whether there was still something missing. Then they beseeched him to create gods who would praise the magnificent achievements and the cosmic order in words and music. Such self-confidence on the part of Pindar and such pretensions are not vain: he fulfills these pretensions in his poetry and, furthermore, is more concerned with his task than with his accomplishments. Pindar is justifiably elated by his intellectual achievement and his success in earning a worthy reputation among a public that he had educated

20. *Nemean,* 5. 20.

to accept exalted pretensions. This achievement is more important than anything else we have considered in preparation for the high social esteem that an intellectual, as we would say, could rely upon in later Greece.

Pindar coined the ideas of his time in the most impressive way. But the same fundamental conceptions are also to be found in other poets who were his contemporaries and whom we usually associate with the philosophers. These were Xenophanes, the earliest, who seems to have written the verses we are concerned with only toward the end of his life of more than ninety years; Parmenides; and finally Empedocles, who was a generation younger than Pindar.

Xenophanes, the Ionian, resembles Pindar in finding fault with the old stories because they relate much that is indecent about the gods—details of "theft, adultery, and deceit." But Xenophanes does not feel the pious awe of the gods that causes Pindar to prefer to remain silent if he comes across something questionable. On the contrary, Xenophanes unmasks the Olympians as anthropomorphic inventions and sends them to Orcus. He also regards a divinity as something sublime. According to him, there is only One God, who is not like a mortal in shape and thought, but who is "all eye, all mind, and all ear." For him, as for Pindar, wisdom (*sophia*) is the highest virtue (*areté*). He separates it from other virtues, as Solon and Tyrtaeus had differentiated their highest virtue from all others. But Xenophanes does not agree at all with Pindar in the things he rejects; in fact, he opposes exactly those ideas with which Pindar had grown up and which he had cherished during all his life. He inveighs against the fact that the victors in different sports contests, whom Pindar praised in his *Epinicia,* have been honored by the citizens.

But he agrees with Pindar in giving high esteem to wisdom and also in ascribing a special wisdom to himself. Yet he does it blatantly, clumsily, and ostentatiously—as Pindar would never have done. Of all those who received honor because of their victories in the games, "no one deserves it so much as *I*, for better than the strength of men and horses is *my* wisdom." Words like these are not found in older poetry; neither Solon nor Tyrtaeus says: *"My* virtue. . . ."

Finally he agrees with Pindar that the wisdom in which he is interested can be found only by searching and striving. "The gods vouchsafed not unto man knowledge of all things from the beginning, but he seeks and in course of time finds out what is better" (frag. 18) . Frag. 10: "Since all have learnt in Homer in the beginning . . ." may be connected with Bacchylides' assertion that man learns from what others have done.

Of course Pindar and Xenophanes are members of opposing factions in their own day. Pindar, in spite of his "new" poetry, is principally conservative. Xenophanes, on the other hand, is radical, progressive, and philosophical. He is firmly resolute about where to take his stand when a conflict arises between beauty and truth. The two poets also differ in their opinions about what wisdom can achieve. With Xenophanes wisdom is largely concerned with what is utilitarian for the city; with Pindar it concerns admiration and praise of the cosmos. Nevertheless, they are united by some fundamental ideas that had been unknown in earlier times.

About Parmenides and Empedocles a few comments should suffice here because their main interests lie outside our topic. Parmenides has deepened the abyss between appearance and truth. He tells—and with that he takes up a subject developed in choral lyrics—how a chariot carries him up to the realm of true cognition in the company of divine beings and how he finds himself there outside the paths of ordinary people (frag. 1). But then again he speaks of the "paths of seeking" (frag. 2. 2). All this reminds us of Pindar. If Parmenides identifies Thinking with Being, it is very obvious that for him, despite a vivid account of divine influence, the human mind is an active mind.

Empedocles provides the most extreme example of the wise man's self-confidence in these times. He regards himself not merely as a "divine prophet," as Bacchylides does, but plainly says (frag. 112. 4): "My friends, I greet you. . . . But I walk amongst you as immortal god, no longer a mortal, honored by all as it becomes me." In a way difficult for us to comprehend, he unites within himself the medicine man, the shaman, and the empirical scientist. He too is acquainted with searching endeavor, but only as a task for *other* people (frag. 114): "The whole cannot be seen nor be heard nor be grasped with the mind by man, but you [he is speaking to a friend and pupil] will try it now since you have separated [from ordinary people], but will not achieve more than to what human thought [*mētis*] can rise." With this strange fellow it may be enough to note that even he, in spite of his claim to divine inspiration, knows something about the mind, which *searches* for truth. However important he was and however much he contributed to the beginnings of science and medicine, he would have seemed quite ridiculous at the end of the fifth century in Athens.

5

TRAGEDY

❖ ❖ ❖

THE archaic lyric poets of Greece laid the foundations for our modern interpretation of man. The Attic tragedians of the fifth century B.C. in turn built upon this base and achieved what we have regarded ever since then as natural and, in general, human. Indeed, we now take for granted that man consists of body and soul. Since historical development has also proceeded on its own way since then, our conception of man is in many respects different from that of classical Greece. Nevertheless, everything from this point onward seems much more familiar to us—as, for example, the statues of classical sculptors appear to be closer and more natural to us. Now we no longer need to exert as much effort and reflection, as we formerly did in order to identify ourselves with something strange.

This is sufficient reason for satisfying ourselves now with a few illustrations. But there are other reasons why we can express ourselves more concisely when speaking about tragedy. Most of the early lyric poets are preserved only in fragments

72

that had to be placed in their proper context before they could be interpreted; but now we are concerned with coherent and completely preserved dramas of the three great tragedians—Aeschylus, Sophocles, and Euripides. Also, Greek tragedies much more than lyric poems belong to the well-established possession of modern man. Poets from ancient times to our own have repeatedly adapted them to their own use, and scholars have often commented on them. Finally, literary and social development at this stage no longer proceeds so impetuously that a differentiated analysis of individual points is necessary to understand the comprehensive picture.

First it is necessary to determine as precisely as possible wherein the image of man as depicted in tragedy differs from the earlier one. E. R. Dodds, in his book *The Greeks and the Irrational,* entitles his second chapter: "From Shame-Culture to Guilt-Culture," borrowing these terms from American anthropologists.[1] The words of his chapter heading characterize a development of moral behavior that has fundamentally altered man's relation to society.

With Homer shame (*aidōs*) regulates the attitude of man to his fellow man. Each individual considers whether or not his reputation, his authority, or his honor has been injured. In later times, however, behavior is determined by a consciousness of guilt. Dodds shows convincingly that in the archaic age a feeling of guilt was spreading and that men believed they were at the mercy of divine power. It is interesting to note, incidentally, that in Greek thought guilt and lack of power are not so closely associated as in Christianity, where weakness and sin virtually coincide.

1. Dodds, p. 26, n. 106 quotes Ruth Benedict, *The Chrysanthemum and the Sword,* pp. 222ff.

In the archaic era, as we have seen, man discovered new possibilities for himself and thereby not only strengthened his self-confidence but, on the other hand, also widened the gap between himself and the absolute. Dodds himself emphasizes that the development of guilt consciousness is a long process. According to the degree of religious feeling, intellectual aspiration, and social pretension, people experience in very different ways the threatening predominance of the divinity. In the social problems with which we have been concerned, this fact as yet has not come to the foreground.

But in Attic tragedy, to which we turn now, the concept of guilt decidedly changes, though some of the new ideas began to appear earlier and some of the old ones survive. The new interpretation of guilt, a deeper and more precise one, now also has an influence upon all Greek thought concerning society.

A society founded on shame and reputation can function only if people have clearly defined ideas about what is right and proper. Only then can everyone accept the judgment of society. We have traced how in archaic times social ties loosen as individuals supplant the traditionally recognized values with more "mental" or "spiritual" ones, how new groups arise that feel intrinsically united, and how single persons dedicated to the quest of truth claim to be superior to their fellow men. The fundamental attachment of all these poets to the "old" culture is evident from the fact that, after all, they believe they have achieved their knowledge through revelation and that they postulate one value as certain and immovable even though it may be attained only with great effort and special grace. Particularly revealing is the characteristic way in which the metaphor of light is generally used. Even for Pindar everything valuable is brightly gleaming; for

Parmenides the journey to truth leads "from the house of night into light," and so forth.

Aeschylus for the first time shows us situations in which one can no longer appeal to traditional values and in which it becomes absurd to care about one's reputation. This occurs when a man is forced to make a choice between two contradictory claims, each of which is sanctioned by a god. Orestes finds himself in such a situation when he is ordered by Apollo to avenge his father, but such vengeance, of course, requires killing his mother. In a similar case King Pelasgos in the *Suppliant Maidens* is obliged to protect the Danaids sitting at the altar but in doing so hurls his city into war against the sons of Aegyptus. In a magnificent monologue (v.407ff.) he thinks "into the depths" in order to arrive at a decision. By producing such scenes and revolving them in his mind, Aeschylus achieves a new concept of human action. Its core is the personal decision; here it no longer helps to ask how an action will be judged by others but only to ask whether or not it is right. In this situation it must be admitted, the feeling of searching and investigating loses its touch of enthusiasm and instead becomes something like a heavy burden. Justice, virtue, and truth can no longer be conceived as objects of the outer world under the image of something bright and gleaming.

In the first great choral lyric of *Agamemnon* the chorus prays to Zeus (v.160ff.):

Zeus: whatever he may be, if this name pleases him in invocation, thus I call upon him. I have pondered everything yet I cannot find a way, only Zeus, to cast this dead weight of ignorance finally from out my brain. . . . Zeus who guided men to think, who has laid it down that wisdom comes alone through suffering. Still there drips in sleep against the heart grief of memory;

against our pleasure we are temperate. From the gods who sit in grandeur grace comes somehow violent [translated by R. Lattimore].

Musing and brooding, man tries to grasp with his thought the loftiest concept that bears the name of Zeus and yet is more than what men ordinarily call Zeus. The aim of investigation has become still more unfathomable ("I have pondered everything, but can find nothing comparable") than, for instance, with Pindar; and therefore the mental endeavor to track it is still more urgent.

The deepest insight at which Aeschylus arrives in this respect is expressed in the phrase "Wisdom through suffering" (*pathei mathos*) . For that expression he reworks an old proverb: "one learns through sad experience." But the meaning of Aeschylus is quite different from what a Homeric hero means when he advises his opponent to leave the field "before he suffers harm: a fool grows wise through experience" [2] and also different from what Hesiod says in almost the same words when referring to the inevitable victory of justice.[3] Here the lesson is: whoever is wise can save himself from unfortunate experience. However, with Aeschylus there is no other way to insight except through suffering, even though we set our minds against it. The point of the proverb is that in retrospect one recognizes the folly of certain actions; in the *Agamemnon* the point is that one is transplanted out of one way of life, out of confident action, into another, into bitter and yet consolatory knowledge.

Sophocles' *Antigone* ends with these words: "Our happiness depends on wisdom all the way. The gods must have

2. *Iliad,* 17. 32, which may be compared with 20. 198.
3. *Works and Days,* 219.

their due. Great words by men of pride bring greater blows upon them. So wisdom comes to the old."

Oedipus Rex of Sophocles depicts in the clearest and most magnificent way how a man is led into insight out of confidence in his own actions—and out of a well-justified confidence, because by solving the riddle of the Sphinx he proved himself especially wise. All his searching and investigation destroys Oedipus himself. This is ultimate wisdom.

An inner change in the life of man had not been represented in earlier literature. Of course, from the beginning one could admonish someone to change his way of life, but that meant only abstaining from evil so that what remained would be good. In this sense Hesiod reproaches his brother with the proverb "one learns through sad experience." In a similar sense, too, Achilles changes his mind at the end of the *Iliad:* he has learned that he himself brought about what happened through his own stubbornness. But that does not mean that from now on he will lead a life essentially different from that which he led before his wrath. In tragedy the issue is that man changes fundamentally in mind and soul. Later a word was found for this alteration: *metanoia,* change of mind, which appears for the first time in Thucydides (3. 36, 4) and in the sense of "repentance, contrition, and conversion" has become significant for Christianity. Aeschylus for the first time sees mind and soul in such a way that this development becomes possible.

Such an alteration in the way of life is known to Aeschylus also in quite a different form—in an untragical, burlesque sphere. In the satyric drama *Isthmiastai* the satyrs leave the service of Dionysus and run away to Poseidon. But these two divine claims do not bring about a tragic conflict, as in the case of Orestes and Pelasgos. The satyrs are simply fed up

with leading the miserable life of uncivilized beings in out-
door nature and want, like the *jeunesse dorée,* to take part
in sports competitions at the Isthmus. In this loose, carefree
world it becomes all the more apparent that men have become more mobile and active, that greater possibilities are
open to one's own initiative.

When the old lyric poets enumerated different ways of life,
they did not take into consideration that a man might veer
from one to another or that he might choose freely between
them. Semonides in a long iambus (7) specifies different kinds
of women, but their types are rigidly fixed according to the
animal from which each one of them is descended. Tyrtaeus
(frag. 9) gives a catalogue of different virtues and abilities
(*aretai*) , but when he postulates courage as the only virtue,
he does not say that one must give up his other virtues. Instead he stresses, according to the tenets of shame-culture,
that the highest fame (*doxa*) lies in courage. The other *aretai*
cannot be chosen freely but rather are gifts that fall to a
man's share—for example, beauty, eloquence, abilities in
sports, royal power, or wealth. Solon enumerates different occupations by which one can earn his living—which certainly
can be freely chosen—but beside them he places others that
different gods have taught to men. Yet the idea that a man
can shift from one to another and, moreover, that they may
have different intrinsic meanings lies outside his consideration.

How new the change from activity to recognition is in
tragedy becomes clear if we recollect how in earlier days the
active man was contrasted with the knowing man. Something that corresponds to this opposition first appeared when
the brave Ajax and the wise Odysseus contended for the
arms of Achilles. It became even more apparent when Pindar

contrasted the man who does great deeds with the man who recognizes and praises them, and when he showed how each one, though great in his own way, is dependent upon the other. But a man could no more transform himself from one to the other than Ajax and Odysseus could.

The comparison with Pindar can show something else: his "great mind," which made him capable of the highest achievement attainable by man—that is, tracking the truth—was a rare grace of the gods. Nothing of this exaltation is felt by Aeschylus. What concerns him is accessible to every man. It is the privilege and duty of every individual, if he discovers himself in an appropriate situation, to ponder by himself and to find out personally what is right. Here the two pillars of Attic and of future democratic society become visible: freedom and justice.

How the conceptions of possible ways of life develop further in the poetry of the fifth century B.C. can be shown in two plays by Euripides. In one play he places in opposition a man whose life is preoccupied with theory and intellectual pursuits and another man who represents practical motivation. In yet another instance the dramatist contrasts the defender of justice with the advocate of power.

In both cases two brothers dispute with one another in long controversial arguments. In the *Antiope,* of which only fragments are preserved, Zethos, a shepherd, pleads for sober, practical goals. Amphion, on the other hand, is devoted to music and defends intellectual as well as theoretical interests. In the *Phoenissae* the sons of Oedipus, Eteocles and Polyneices, quarrel with one another.

From the *Antiope* Plato in his *Gorgias* has fortunately preserved just such verses in the speech of Zethos which can well be compared with passages from earlier poets whom I have previously discussed. Zethos reproaches his brother for vanity and love of prestige: [4] "Everyone shines in that work and pursues it, spending the greatest part of the day in it, for which he finds in himself the strongest abilities." Then soon afterward appear the verses: [5] "You start an evil thing by introducing this Muse, the lazy, wine-loving, who neglects possessions." We see that Zethos presupposes and disapproves of the fact that everyone tries, according to his own capabilities, to find a life by which he may achieve a reputation. At first this sounds like a quotation from Tyrtaeus. People win fame (*doxa*) according to their *aretai,* and *aretē* to a great extent is a "gift" like beauty, strength, eloquence; and such capacities determine the *bios,* the way of life. But one thing not mentioned by Tyrtaeus or by any other earlier poet is that someone adapts his life to his own abilities. This comes out even more clearly in another portion ascribed to the same speech by Dodds in his commentary on the *Gorgias* (p.277): "You neglect what you ought to consider [and to look after]. For though you have acquired for your portion such a noble nature of the soul [*psychês physin*], you proceed vainly in a womanish attire [that refers to the long garment of a musician] . . . neither in speech, that is, before a court or in politics, will you achieve anything useful . . . nor in war."

Zethos attributes to his brother "a noble nature of the soul." And that causes us to recall that Pindar claimed to have a "great mind," which according to his belief he possessed "by nature." But Pindar's "great mind" is, so to speak, directed outward: it aims at the great objects worthy of praise; whereas here the "noble nature of the soul" is the personal interior out of which an individual can shape the

4. Frag. 183, ed. Nauck.
5. Frag. 184 and frag. adespotum 395.

different possible forms of his life. The activity of the soul is more conspicuous here than in any of the passages discussed previously.

Very little is preserved of the speech in which Amphion replies. Actually he praises the "inactive man" (frag. 193) ; yet he emphasizes that the way of life he defends is more useful for the state (frag. 194). Thus he does not yet conceive of "theory" in its pure form but still accepts the hypothesis of his adversary that the public weal is the proper guide to conduct, just as Xenophanes had recommended his "wisdom" by declaring it to be the greatest advantage to the *polis*. In another fragment (910) from an unknown tragedy—perhaps from a choral lyric of the *Antiope*—Euripides describes "theory" in a purer state, but even here the utility for the citizens enters in: "Happy he who has learnt investigation and is not going to harm his fellow citizens or do injustice but contemplates the unchangeable order of immortal nature, what it consists of and how it is composed." For Pindar too the highest aim was to recognize the order of the cosmos, and his self-confidence in face of the active and mighty person depended upon this "wisdom." But for Euripides it is a question of "investigation" (*historia*), not in order to praise beauty but to find out in detail how the objects of heaven and earth are constructed. Now the active mind has become free for science and philosophy and independent of all other interests—free even from poetry. It is characteristic of the time that this choral lyric does not praise a person because he takes part in something divine or call him fortunate because he is on the side of active people, but instead it praises the wise man, who in the time of Pindar was the one who did the praising.

Later Plato (for example, in the *Theaetetus*) develops an

even purer conception of what is "theoretical," and ever since then there have been discussions of the relative merits of the *vita activa* and the *vita contemplativa.*

In Plato's *Gorgias* Callicles, in trying to strengthen his own position before Socrates, uses the words of Zethos not so much in order to defend practice against theory but in order to affirm the claim of might against that of right. This conflict is carried out by Eteocles and Polyneices in Euripides' *Phoenician Women.* As their mother Iocaste tries to reconcile the hostile brothers, Eteocles begins his speech about the right of the stronger (v.499ff.) with a thought that we have encountered again and again wherever poets reveal new fields of the mind. He speaks in favor of "truth" as opposed to conventional opinions. But how different truth looks here: "If all men saw the fair and wise the same, men would not have debaters' double strife. But nothing is like or even among men except the name they give—which is not the fact. I'll speak to you, Mother, without concealment" [translated by Elizabeth Wyckoff].

The opposition of a mere word and the fact or reality itself has served ever since Solon (frag. 8. 7f.) to unmask the man who employs pretty words. But Euripides uses it from his earliest days (and we shall encounter a passage from the *Alcestis* later) in order to contrast true reality and mere appearance. Eteocles reveals what he thinks is the true nature of man: "I'd go to the stars beyond the eastern sky or under earth, if I could do one thing, seize tyranny, the greatest of the gods." At the end of the speech he says: "If one must do a wrong, it's best to do it pursuing power—otherwise, let's have virtue." What people call morals is nothing but cowardice and weakness. The good is power (cf. v.507f.). This radical unmasking of the traditional values that through Callicles in Plato's *Gorgias* and Thrasymachus in Plato's *Republic* has come down to Nietzsche is possible only because Eteocles knows himself to be capable of deciding through his own thinking what is good and what is evil. But his confidence in his own mind, in its own potentialities, so to speak, goes even further. The "nature of one's own soul" and its force constitute the only reality in the social life of men.

We will not delve into the moral implications that arise out of such utterances nor into the question of how old Homeric ideas about *areté* and heroic egotism have been developed here in a one-sided and distorted way, since the regulating norm of all shame culture, the consideration of respect and reputation in society, has now been abolished. I merely wish to make clear that this radical and conscious immorality becomes possible only at a time when one recognizes in the human mind something "abstract," which can serve as the origin of actions and be a "prime mover," if we may apply this Aristotelean phrase in a world deprived of gods. This is the reverse of that mental freedom praised by Euripides as the happiness of intellectual life.

In addition to the faculty of acting for itself, we found as the second force of an abstract mind the faculty of uniting several people. This capacity also appears in a new form with Euripides since he shows us how men can be bound together with a new intensity of feeling.

Even in the earliest of his surviving dramas, the *Alcestis*, he stresses the point that living together in one house must be "true" and "real," that the *philoi* must be "genuine" relatives and friends. When Alcestis hears that her husband Admetus must die unless someone else will die for him, she sacrifices her life for him. Therefore she is for Admetus the only one who will ever be called his wife (v.329ff.). His aged parents, on the other hand, who do not lay down their lives for him were *philoi* only according to the word (*logōi*) but not in fact and truth (*ergōi*, v.339). His father Pheres was not his father in the genuine and right way (*orthôs*), Admetus tells him (v.636).

In the early archaic age, it was important for Archilochus and Alcaeus that a friend be a "true" friend, because in the new self-created communities of that time and especially in political groups and parties, perjury and treason were the cardinal crimes. For Euripides marriage is by no means such an arbitrarily founded union, but he takes wedlock in the old conventional sense. Something has changed, however. Odysseus, in wishing Nausicaa a happy marriage, implied that a married couple ought to harm their enemies and be useful to their friends. That sounded as though marriage were, like a political club, a union of common interests. But if for Euripides the reliable partner becomes important in marriage, it is not because the family must stick together before friend and foe. In an entirely new way he surveys marriage on the basis of what it could be and what it ought to be. As a result "good husband" or "bad wife" acquires another meaning.

Of course a certain behavior had always been expected of the members of a family. Helen, who left husband and children, or, certainly, Clytaemnestra, who committed adultery and slew her husband, have always been considered bad wives. But they did not pretend to be anything else. Admetus and Pheres accomplish what one usually expects from a husband or a father; in any case, they themselves regard their behavior as proper. Yet neither one is a "real" father or a "real" husband.

Here, too, as in the speech of Eteocles, Euripides makes use of the opposition of "the word" and "reality" in order to reveal the true, proper nature, though not for the reason that he does so much later in his *Phoenician Women*—to unmask pretentious words or deprive man of his illusions. In his earliest surviving drama he uses the contrast for what one might call just the opposite reason; he follows the method by which the old lyric poets tried to track the true value concealed behind conventional ideas. Yet for him this true nature is not something gleaming and ostensibly objective, as beauty was for Sappho, nor to be sure as truth was for Pindar or Parmenides—that is, something separated from ordinary mortals by an abyss and tracked down only by the grace of some god. Being a real friend here is achieved by the simple, quiet Alcestis. It is something domestic, intimate, and internal. That may remind us of Sappho, who is much less pretentious than the other poets. But through a comparison with her we see the essential difference. Alcestis fulfills a task that is assigned to her by her traditional position in the house. What she is provides her with a goal. She sees it and acknowledges it.

We know little about the myth of Alcestis prior to Euripides, only that Alcestis, who gives her life for her husband, originally was a figure of a fairy tale. In fairy tales and myths there have always been such moving, beautiful, and noble beings. But as Kurt von Fritz has shown [6] Euripides suddenly takes this sublime, glorified figure as a standard and applies it to everyday reality. For him the fairy tale becomes a moral demand. No wonder that all except Alcestis now look miserable. The fairy tale shows the beautiful picture of a single great deed but does not draw any ethical conclusions for a genuine conjugal life. There we accept the extraordinary deed of an extraordinary person without taking into

6. *Antike und Abendland*, 5, 1956, 27ff.

account that in fact all the persons concerned are equal and that we could expect the same from each one of them. But Euripides confronts each individual with the same question —to what extent he lives only for himself and to what extent he also lives for the family. He is aware of what "real" and "true" living together means. Even if marriage according to sober Attic law is an institution designed to bring legitimate children into the world, that certainly does not prevent a married couple from being deeply attached to one another. Euripides sees the mental ties in a new light. If this union of the souls, which evolves out of a primitive cohabitation, becomes the vital element in marriage, then those problems and conflicts arise that Euripides has in mind.

Whoever in earlier times spoke of a good friend or of a good spouse was concerned only with whether in an isolated instance someone would not prove unfaithful, commit adultery, or break the oath of friendship—that is, whether he was *not* a *bad* friend. Euripides asks who is a true friend in the same way that Simonides had asked who is a good man. Thus he pushes the genuine friend out of the ordinary, commonplace world into an ideal sphere which human beings cannot live up to.

And yet they can learn to live up to it in a very human way. In his *Heracles* Euripides describes how all heroism leads only to terror and disaster. At the time when Heracles fulfills his last and most difficult labor by going to Hades to fetch Cerberus, the usurper Lycus in Thebes tries to kill his kin—his aged father Amphitryon, his wife Megara, and his children. Heracles comes back just in time to prevent this slaughter. But then he is overcome by madness, and he himself slays his own wife and children. All this happens, as the gods' messenger Iris has predicted (v.841f.), to prevent the belief from arising that after the heroic deeds of Heracles the gods became nothing and that humans could achieve greatness without having to atone.

When Heracles later becomes conscious of his terrible deed and realizes his situation, he wants to take his own life. At this moment Theseus, his friend and king of Athens, whom Heracles had once rescued from Hades, enters. "I have come because I feel *with* you your sorrow," Theseus says (*synalgōn ēlthon,* 1204). "I don't object to sharing your misfortune [*syn ge soi prassein kakōs*] for once I was happy with you [1220] . . . I loathe a friend whose gratitude grows old, a friend who takes his friend's prosperity but will not voyage with him [*symplein*] in his grief" (translated by W. Arrowsmith).

Thus he persuades Heracles to live on and takes him with him to Athens. Heracles begs Theseus to fulfill one task with him (*synkamnein,* 1386) before going there and to bring with him (*synkātástēson,* 1387) Cerberus to Argos. Then he asks the Thebans to lament with him (*sympenthēsate,* 1390). To his old father he says: "In spite of all that has happened, compel your soul to bear misfortune with me [*sympherein,* 1366]."

In this survey of the last scene of the *Heracles* I have used exclusively those quotations having compounds with *syn-*. This shows sufficiently the great importance attached to the idea of being together, acting together, and feeling together. We might also have shown how significant the compounds with *syn-* (*synoiken, sympherein, syntlēnai, synkamnein, synalgein, synnikān*) are for the ideas developed in the *Alcestis;* and the same is true for other tragedies of Euripides, in which these compounds first become numerous. The end of the *Heracles* makes especially clear what common experiences mean for Euripides and what is new about them. Theseus explains to Heracles his human situation (1314ff.) : "Fate exempts no man; all men are flawed," and in a most remarkable way he continues: ". . . and so the gods, unless the poets lie./Do not the gods commit adultery?/Have they not cast their fathers into chains,/in pursuit of power? Yet all the same,/despite their crimes, they live upon Olympos./How dare you then, mortal that you are,/to protest your fate, when the gods do not?"

After the entire development of Greek thinking has resulted in lifting ever higher what is good and right and has made an ideal of it, then man recognizes that he must resign himself to the fact that men, and even the gods, are entangled in guilt. From the early days onward it was taken for granted by the Greeks that men are mortal and frail, that they make mistakes and fall into error. But only from the time that man assumes full responsibility for his actions, as the tragedians have revealed it, does the consciousness of frailty become an awareness of guilt. This awareness becomes so urgent with Euripides that he for the first time speaks of a bad conscience (*Orestes,* 396: *synesis*) . Even the gods, says Theseus—though Heracles of course contradicts him (1341ff.) —have to resign themselves to being guilty.

This is the beginning of a new humanity which, as we shall see later, stamps its image on the society of the New Comedy. As early as the *Alcestis* an act of friendship restores order: Heracles proves to be a true friend and brings Alcestis back into the light. In the *Heracles* Theseus draws the conclusion out of a situation brought about by human shortcomings and says (1337) : "Now you need friends." And the drama concludes with the words of the aged Amphitryon: "He who prefers wealth and power to good friends is a fool." Heracles is comforted not by a belief in the gods, who, as Aeschylus and Sophocles taught, maintain order in the world despite all human suffering, but instead by human friendship.

As always, a new feeling of belonging together implies a new sentiment of loneliness. All the three great tragedians know the loneliness of the guilty: Prometheus and Orestes, Ajax and Oedipus, Admetus and Heracles are all, because of their actions and an awareness of what they have done, lonelier than men could ever previously have been. Self-recognition drags them out of a society in which they have been active. In the later tragedies of Euripides men are even lonelier.

Alone, at night, on the seashore (that is, in the landscape that from the very beginning of poetry has been associated with solitude) Agamemnon wanders about in the beginning of the *Iphigenia in Aulis*, a pitiful hero, in utter helplessness because he does not know whether he should sacrifice his daughter Iphigenia in order to secure the success of the expedition against Troy. This is one of the most impressive scenes of ancient tragedy, but also one of the most horrible, though it contains nothing of the bloodshed and terror to which other tragedies have accustomed us. Here we are concerned with the inner destruction of a man. Agamemnon weeps; he envies his old slave, who comes out of the tent, because he leads a life free from danger and from the burden of honor and fame.

Unfortunately I cannot discuss the entire scene here—how Agamemnon through lies has become involved in this shameful situation, how he wavers in his decisions, and fails in a world that has become meaningless. When his brother Menelaus enters the scene, the two men reveal only one trait in common: each tries mercilessly to expose the other. Each one shows that the other's actions are only cowardice, weakness, and cheap egotism. And yet, miserable as they are, both arouse our compassion. Euripides reveals something in them that in this age of disillusionment remains fascinatingly human—the same thing that Heracles too had experienced as ultimately human and to which Theseus had stooped in friendship.

Euripides is the first poet who, according to what is told about him, sought solitude for himself. He withdrew, as his biographer reports, from the multitude to Salamis into a cave overlooking the sea.[7]

7. Schwartz, E., *Scholia in Euripidem*, vol. 1, pp. 4, 23, Berlin, 1881; cf. Aulus Gellius, 15. 20.

6

COMEDY AND HELLENISTIC POETRY

❖ ❖ ❖

THE development of Greek thought from Homer to the
lyric poets of the late archaic period follows a course that
few would hesitate to regard as one of continuous progress.
Throughout the ages certainly there have always been people
who considered the Homeric poems as the greatest of poetical
achievements. But that does not mean they could immediately identify themselves with the figures of the *Iliad*
and the *Odyssey*. We can easily show that, whenever men
have assumed such identification, they have done so through
a romantic misunderstanding. The loving attachment to
Homer, if it is not merely an aesthetic admiration, is a longing for lost youth, for the greatness of a historical dawn that
can never be recovered.

Homer depicted a world that was great and coherent in itself. He could do justice to all the requirements of his time,
and what he said cannot be expressed in any other way.
When, for instance, he described the way in which Athena

restrained Achilles from an indiscreet action, we inevitably
lose something if we interpret this scene as an "inner" psychological state described in a primitive way by introducing
a god. Of course, the gods were more than we can explain by
psychology—even by our depth psychology. We cannot identify ourselves with the world of Homer—partly because we
cannot revive artificially the belief in Homeric gods, and also
because all his ideas were given to him by tradition. For him
there was as yet no possibility of selecting ideas freely. So we
too are not at liberty to choose.

This situation changes with tragedy, and especially with
Euripides. When different ways of life become open to choice,
one way is inevitably regarded as better and the other as
worse. And since Greek tragedy almost reaches that analytical
understanding of man which has remained valid for later
times, the decisions to choose either this or that life confront
us also with the question: what do we sanction? Admittedly
Pindar was aware that he sang a "new song." But only since
Euripides has there been consciousness of a "new life." Only
since then has there been a "modern spirit" as opposed to an
"old-fashioned" one. And only since then has there been a
contest over whether the old or the new way of life is prefer-
able.

Especially have subsequent generations disputed an issue
that was problematic with Euripides—namely, is this growing sense of freedom and realization of choice really a blessing
to mankind? Scarcely anyone will question the benefits derived from the freeing of man's theoretical intellect for research or doubt the good accruing from increased personal
and interior relations among men. Nor, on the other hand,
will many fail to deplore that the desire for power has become uninhibited, that many moral restraints have been re-

laxed, and that man has lapsed into insecurity and is tormented by nihilism. But of course one is not allowed to separate these two aspects from each other. Both are necessary consequences of the newly acquired concept of the human mind.

The comedies of Aristophanes thrust us into the midst of this dispute. Indeed they even derive sustenance from the fact that they introduce onto the stage completely new, unheard of, and fantastic possibilities of life. Furthermore, they repeatedly consider what is inadequate and insubstantial in our society and question how man can replace what exists with something better and more beautiful.

Of course people have always imagined a better life, in peace and concord, without worries about daily bread, and they have usually either placed a golden age at the beginning of human history or have hoped for a better future—if after death on the islands of the blessed. Besides such mythological fictions about a blissful life either lost or to be hoped for, there are, as far as I know, only two early Greek poems in which the poet freely follows his creative imagination—an approach that seems quite commonplace to us. The *skolion* of Bacchylides for the Macedonian King Alexander, son of Amyntas, describes how "the heart of noble youths is warmed by the sweet compulsion of the swift-circling cup." Then they hope for love, for the capture of towns, for monarchy, gold and ivory, wheat-laden ships that bring great wealth from Egypt. A similar drinking-song by Pindar (frag. 124 a/b) tells how "boon-companions sail to the open sea and come to an unreal [*pseudē*] coast." If Aristophanes in his comedies produces a world of happiness, of wealth, of peace, of fair hopes fully realized, he differs from such early dreams by showing also the hard political and social reality of his time, the sor-

rows of the Peloponnesian war and of the crumbling
Athenian empire. When he builds up his cheerful scenes, as
opposed to this gloomy background, he not only surrenders
himself to his burlesque fancy but also uses the new capacities
of a free mind by admitting deliberately subtilized construc-
tions. He builds up utopias.

During the following centuries such utopias become the
classical form for developing political and social theories. It
may suffice to recall Plato's *Republic*. By this time the element of fancy and dream has receded even further in favor
of arbitrary rational construction. Here too philosophy has
taken the place of poetry.

For a moment let us consider an instance in which
Aristophanes begins to criticize the society and the politics of
his time. It seems to me that he criticizes institutions, political
programs, and social conditions much less than is usually
supposed; nevertheless he certainly criticizes well-defined
human shortcomings and above all those that had come to the
fore through the recent development of man's interpretation
of man. However this may be, Aristophanes again and again
takes as the target of his derision those occupations which in
former days had produced the most distinguished representatives of the intellect.

The gayest and purest utopia of Aristophanes exists in his
Birds. When the new *polis* of the birds, the "Cloud-cuckoo-
town," has happily been founded, some unpleasant guests
(v.904ff.) who appear and try to derive profit from the new
settlement have to be chased away by whipping. First comes
a poet, then an oracle-monger, then Meton—the famous as-
tronomer, scheduler of calendars, and mathematician—after
him a commissioner (*episkopos*) who has to establish the
constitutions in subjugated cities, and finally a "statute-

seller" who wants to huckster "new laws." Poet, seer, scientist, legislator—all had formerly borne the honorary title of "wise man," as in fact the poet here is ironically termed (v.934). Not only in the *Birds* but in other comedies as well, such "wise men" have lost their old dignity for Aristophanes because their wisdom is no longer "true" and "real." For him they are *alazónes*, chatterboxes, busybodies, or tattlers. Here the oracle-monger and Meton are called by this name, as Socrates is in the *Clouds* (cf. 102. 449. 1494); and if in the *Frogs* Euripides gives this name to Aeschylus (909. 919), then this is but the impudence of Euripides, to whom Aeschylus replies (1069): "You have taught the citizens to prattle and babble."

After all we have learned from Euripides it is easy to understand why Aristophanes applies the word *alazónes* to the representatives of those professions that formerly were considered wise and that laid claim to wisdom for themselves. We found that there was a tendency throughout earlier poetry to take seriously words like "beautiful," "friendly," "good" and so to find out what, in opposition to the ordinary meaning of the words, actually constitutes true beauty, true friendship, and true virtue. This tendency had come to a head with Euripides. In the *Alcestis,* for instance, he had shown that men are not conscious of what such words demand from them or, as happened with Agamemnon in the *Iphigenia in Aulis,* they cannot realize the true meaning even though they know it.

The *alazónes* of Aristophanes, the babblers and busybodies, are simplifications and caricatures of such modern and broken existences as we became acquainted with in Euripides. Aristophanes looks upon them as though they are nothing but vain and intentional frauds. In fact, he cannot do otherwise if he wishes to have the laughter on his own side. But by selecting so effectively these *faux-monnayeurs,* these counterfeiters, from among the modern "wise men," he puts his finger on a wound of his time.

With this kind of derision Aristophanes does not do justice either to Socrates or to Euripides. In fact, Euripides and Socrates themselves did nothing but try to combat this illusion of folly and vanity. But they became suspect because only at the stage of reflection reached by Socrates and especially by Euripides did the loss of natural simplicity and naive self-confidence become obvious. This is the main reason that Euripides is so much more important for Aristophanes than all the earlier tragedians. So he ridicules Euripides bitterly.

About a hundred years later the New Comedy harvests the same fields once tilled by Euripides, but the fruits are very different. Last year the first complete comedy of Menander, the best dramatist of the so-called New Comedy, was published after having been discovered in Egypt. At the very beginning of this play, the *Dyscolos* (that is, the grumbler or misanthrope), there are some motifs that we first encountered with Euripides. In the prologue the god Pan refers to the *dyscolos,* the principal character of the comedy, as an *apánthropos ánthropos* (v.6), an inhuman human being. He is a non-man because he does not speak to his fellow men in a friendly manner and, full of distrust, withdraws from everybody.

You remember that according to Tyrtaeus a man was one who possessed the virtue of bravery and who devoted all his efforts to the state, if necessary sacrificing his own life. By this time and especially in the late archaic period the virtue of the intellect—wisdom (*sophía*)—had become more promi-

nent among other virtues, and the aim that raised man beyond himself was recognition of truth. In some authors of
the third century B.C. *anthropos,* man, is no longer seen as
opposite to god but to animal, and so the word *anthropos*
comes to mean a being with *logos,* with intellect. But it is
true that in late tragedy we already find a countercurrent.
Agamemnon in the beginning of the *Iphigenia in Aulis* is a
man whom reflection deprives of naive confidence in his own
actions, and Euripides more than once speaks of the danger
of someone who is "all too wise." But I cannot pursue this
subject any further. In any event, Menander does not think
of these old virtues or of mental capacities when he speaks
simply of *anthropos* or man.

In the New Comedy there is nothing left that could give
man a goal beyond his own personal life. There is no longer
a state that could provide worthy tasks since the Macedonians
have occupied the cities that once were autonomous. Striving
for knowledge has fallen to the share of philosophers and
specialists in different fields. The queries of good and evil
have now become "theoretical," and the schools of philosophers quibble over them. Thus poetry does not create new
groups. The idea that poetry, even if it has lost much of its
old content, can have its own realm of beauty and that new
cliques become possible among "literary" people is not discovered until a generation later.

What, then, do human and inhuman mean for Menander,
and what sort of public does he address and depict in his
comedies?

We have seen how the old traditional groups, such as
family, clan, and army, were thought to have been instituted
by the gods. But in the course of Greek history they lost their
original importance, and new communities arose—such as

political parties, states, religious congregations, and philosophical schools—all founded upon spiritual principles. Tragedy, before the background of the democratic *polis,* had posed the great questions of justice, guilt, freedom, and different ways of life. Even Aristophanes was still concerned with them. And we felt ourselves dragged into discussions concerning our own vital decisions so that even we had to take a definite stand.

Since this mental attitude (or call it ideology) and the higher goals (or superstructures) now disappear, there remains what we call in the strict sense of the word "society," a society that merely lives together but is not united by common aims or interests. In such surroundings personal convictions easily acquire the appearance of a vulgar obtrusion or a ridiculous pomposity and pretension (*alazonia*). For Menander *anthropos* signifies the man who fits into such a society.

In this society too the Greeks prove to be sufficiently gifted to create exemplary poetical forms. The domestic comedies of Menander and his contemporaries are the ancestors of the Roman plays by Plautus and Terence; and from these are derived the Renaissance and baroque comedies, modern comedy and domestic tragedy, and even the films of our day. From these plays the Western world has learned what "society" is. The conventions regulating what "one" does (this "one" who is almighty wherever there still is a society) have to a great extent been determined by the New Comedy of the late fourth century B.C. This is of course different from the rigid religious convictions or ritual schemes of behavior that we find in early times. But here rules gained through experience are laid down as to how people can live together with as little friction as possible. Thus by being free from specific religious, political, and moral obligations, the New Comedy has been enabled to exert its great influence on the social civilization of the Romans and of all western nations. Good behavior can be more easily exported and transplanted than religious rites and moral principles.

The grumbler, the *dyscolos*, in Menander's play lives a solitary life in the country. But he is not forced to do so as was Alcaeus, who had not succeeded in his political plans and therefore was banished. He is at variance with his fellow men and by his own will has withdrawn from them. He has retired, but surely not like Euripides—in order to live for mental activity that raises him above the ordinary crowd. It is simply his character that prevents him from getting along with other people. He is a whimsical misconstruction of nature, of which there are so many, and which Theophrastus just about the time of the *Dyscolos* depicted in his *Characters*.

The *Dyscolos* is an early work of the very young Menander. This becomes apparent especially at the end of the play, through the way in which therapeutics are applied to the inhuman man: Menander, splitting the course of treatment into two parts, uses burlesque motifs that savor more of the Old than of the New Comedy. The first cure occurs in the fourth act when the misanthrope falls into a well from which he can be rescued only by the help of somebody else. He then realizes: "I thought that I was self-sufficient and should need no help from anyone. Now, though, having seen clearly that the end of life comes suddenly with no forewarning, I find that my judgment was wrong on that point. I am forced to admit that there must be someone near to give help at any time" (translated by L. A. Post).

Though the *dyscolos* becomes aware that human weakness is dependent upon help—which truth Theseus had taught

Heracles in the tragedy of Euripides—he does not see that one really must be connected with other people. Indeed he does not speak of friendship as Theseus does. This attitude is corrected to a certain degree toward the end of the fifth act. By being whipped, though not too severely, he is induced to take part in the marriages of his son and of his stepson, as well as in the rustic festival in the precinct of Pan. He is threatened with whipping—very much as Thersites was whipped in the *Iliad,* but there are differences. In Homer, Odysseus administered the whipping; in Menander, only a cook and a slave are permitted to do it. In the *Iliad* the purpose was to show drastically that someone lacked reputation or honor; in the *Dyscolos* a comic motif, found also in the *Birds* of Aristophanes, concludes the play with slapstick. But ill-treatment is not an intrinsically satisfying solution, though admittedly it would have been difficult for Menander to find any truly convincing way of leading the misanthrope back to human society. Later Menander solves conflicts in a less naive manner. Yet what he aims at in this play is exactly the same as in his subsequent works.

In his later plays Menander finds what is human in friendship and sympathy and depicts it again and again. Respectful and considerate understanding of one's neighbor is the virtue that Menander's characters exercise; it is also the virtue which Menander himself exercises toward his characters. In his society—a society in a very specialized sense—the ruling mental principle is psychology. And psychology signifies not postulating aims, not fixing morals according to a program, but reckoning only with the simplest and most natural instincts, explaining why something deviates from the normal, and pardoning it through explanation.

Menander's characters are restricted to their narrow private circle. The fact that Alexander has conquered the world and that his successors fight over his inheritance is reflected to the utmost in the New Comedy by a scene in which a soldier enters with a full purse and delivers big speeches. Athens has now become a provincial town and no longer plays a role in world politics. The interests of its people are reduced to the simplest desires: the old care for their possessions; the young live for worldly pleasures. But their spirits are so softened that nothing is pursued any longer with great passion. The old are by no means wild speculators but misers; the young are often incited to action only when under the influence of wine. And, as a rule, if a young man gets into a scrape, only the slaves are active enough to provide help.

The noble and human men in Menander are no longer convinced that they can pursue higher interests. In fact, they no longer believe that there is anything like a great action which makes sense. They prove themselves by respecting their fellow men and enabling human society, taken as it is, to live in harmony. The virtue of these men is philanthropy, love of their fellow men. To it belongs understanding of human frailty—that "nothing human is alien to one." If in Euripides Theseus approached Heracles with this human understanding, his deed was that of a single proven friend. Such psychological response to a neighbor now becomes the moral foundation of society—it is the very opposite of moral rigor.

But psychological tact is expected of man not only with regard to his fellow men but also with regard to himself. In the most sensitive and beautiful comedy of Menander, the *Epitrepontes* or *Arbitrants,* as far as we can trace its actions, all events lead to the point at which a young man realizes exactly what he has done. While drunk he had raped the daughter of a citizen, and afterward he had married her without knowing that she was the girl of the previous encounter. When his wife is about to give birth to a child (ahead of schedule, as he knows), he is enraged with her until he is made to understand that he himself is the only person against whom he can direct his moral indignation. In a case similar to that of Admetus in Euripides, he must realize what his own situation is and that all his grand words are nothing but words. Thus he fulfills the old Delphic exhortation: "Know thyself." Yet he is not a Tantalus, who in wild hubris has violated the boundaries between human and divine power; nor an Oedipus, who in an honest endeavor has trusted his own knowledge; nor even an Admetus, who has not recognized the claim that was laid upon him. He is an innocuous young citizen who, without a plan, without an idea, even without real consciousness because he was drunk, has fallen victim to human weakness.

The greatness of Menander lies in the fact that out of such subject matter, which is really unimportant in itself, he can develop human characters and reactions. I cannot expound here in detail how in the *Epitrepontes* the *hetaera* Habrotonon cleverly and sympathetically plots and resolves the intrigue—and as a slave she is allowed to do that—while at the same time furthering her own interests and winning her freedom. The poet also succeeds in making the spectator experience a psychological understanding and smile cheerfully at this play based on human frailty in a bourgeois society.

In the last phase of distinguished Greek poetry, with Callimachus and his contemporaries, art has become, as we have already observed, an end in itself: art is to be enjoyed as art. But the pretensions of art have grown to such an extent that only a small circle can appreciate them. From the earliest times it was taken for granted by the Greek poets that poetry was sweet and heart-warming. Nevertheless, as we have seen, certain motifs of content had always given impetus to poets: the remembrance of great deeds, the disclosure of truth, the search after virtue, etc. But we have also seen that in the course of time the belief that such aims were attainable by poetry had been lost. These aims developed into meditation, thought, philosophy, and science.

In this situation, during the first half of the third century, a few poets once more succeeded in cultivating a prolific new field—this time the field of "pure poetry." Social conditions for these poets were related in some respects to those of the late archaic period. After the democratic intermezzo, during which tragedy and comedy blossomed in Athens, there were again courts of monarchs, in which the poet had to give evidence of his intellect.

Again the same mental capacities emerge as with the archaic Ionian poets such as Simonides, Ibycus, Bacchylides, and Anacreon—sentimentality and wit, that is a free play of feeling and thought. Compared with these motifs, the moral concerns of Greek poets on the mainland, of the Boeotian Pindar, as well as of the Attic writers of tragedy and comedy, are not prominent. Yet the Athenian heritage is shown in some traits: these Hellenistic poets consciously choose their forms of life and poetry; they even give theoretical reasons for their attitudes. Furthermore, they renounce, as Menander did, all pathos, moral programs, and political engagements. Smiling and understanding, they look upon the demeanor of men.

Four poets of this time are remarkable for us because their verses have survived in sufficient quantity and because they are great enough to utter new ideas clearly and convincingly: Callimachus, Theocritus, Apollonius of Rhodes, and Aratus.

The last two of these I shall omit here: Apollonius in his *Argonautica* takes up the Homeric tradition, and Aratus with his astronomical work resumes the didactic poetry of Hesiod. Thus they aim more at an objective representation, and the personal motifs are not immediately apparent, though they could be shown there too.

What is particularly striking about these poets is that they consider themselves artists. When I compared Pindar's remarks about his "new" poetry with those of Callimachus and how the latter took up the idea and changed it, I mentioned that Pindar (like his contemporaries Xenophanes, Parmenides, and Empedocles) was proud of his wisdom because it revealed new truth. Callimachus also speaks of his own particular wisdom, which elevates him above others, but his *sophia* does not strive for knowledge. In the old *sophia* art had always been contained; now art is the principal value of *sophia*.

Callimachus speaks not only to a small number of *literati* but to a fixed circle of like-minded friends who are bound together by the same aesthetic convictions. He is the first Greek poet who develops a theory about his poetry. Thus he founds a poetical school similar to the philosophical schools which had existed ever since Plato's Academy and which were held together by common philosophical theories. When Sappho or Alcaeus, Tyrtaeus, or Solon united groups through their poetry, they never did so because of common opinions about poetry. When Pindar objected to Simonides and Bacchylides, he was angry about their inadequacies and pretensions, not about their style. And when Euripides argued for the modern ideas of his time, the whole way of life came up for discussion. Aristophanes in his *Frogs* was the first who began to set up a contrast of styles—exalted and base—

derived from the differences of Aeschylus and Euripides. By employing this opposition of styles, Callimachus creates something like a literary clique. Almost the same is true for Theocritus: often the literary discussions of his circle of friends are touched upon in his *Idylls*.

These artistic aspirations, of course, are concerned first of all with form. No one has ever filed his meters with such exquisite taste as Callimachus; nobody has made such enchanting music out of vowels and consonants or has adapted so perfectly the sounds of a poem to its subject matter. But the pretensions of these connoisseurs, who withdraw from practical life and flee into the realm of delicate artistic playing, inevitably influence the subjects of their poems. On the one hand, these poets treat topics which interest the educated and literate: curiosities of mythological and literary tradition, and especially material that enables a poet to sharpen his wit. On the other hand, besides this intellectual pleasure and often interwoven with it, we find something that appeals to the sensitivity of these fastidious *literati*—subjects which are plain, simple, and naive. Theocritus, the inhabitant of a large city, is attracted to the pastoral life; the erudite Callimachus depicts lovingly and understandingly the busy paltriness of old Hecale and the childish babbling of little Artemis. There is a certain irony in the fact that the understanding of the lower classes and of little people is developed in this airy sphere of intellectual play. But we have found the underlying premises for this phenomenon in the *Iphigenia in Aulis*, where Agamemnon, longing to escape a great troubled world, had praised the slave who did not have to bear the burden of reflection and responsibility. This was at the time when people were first learning to regard a slave as a human being. In the meantime the difference between a refined and a simple life had become more acute. Certainly it was not yet as sharp as it became two thousand years later when Marie Antoinette began to play the shepherdess, but the sociological situation was not dissimilar.

The motif of idealized shepherds and pastoral poetry impressively exemplifies the fact that patterns of thought invented by the Greeks have again and again helped men in later times to apprehend their own situation. Herein lies their peculiar immortality. They are always reinterpreted and therewith changed, but they remain effective.

They themselves originated from very definite historical conditions; and we have seen repeatedly that each great form of Greek poetry interacts with a certain stage in man's interpretation of man and with the specific form of society provided by this stage. Conditions evoke ideas and ideas in turn produce the intellectual hypotheses for new social development. Poetry is a creator, a catalyst for change.

It seems to me that by the time of Callimachus and Theocritus another poet has relentlessly come to grips with poetry. But since he does not care to talk about himself and his conceptions of poetry but rather gives objective descriptions, such polemics can be proved only by showing that his poems become alive and meaningful when seen against this background. But that idea, of course, may be fallacious.

In 1891 large portions of the mimes of Herondas were recovered, and a small scrap recently on papyrus. (Mimes are short dramatic scenes that can be compared to skits performed nowadays in night clubs.) During the seventy years that we have possessed pieces of Herondas, they have seldom been appreciated. Generally they are thought to be the tasteless, unimportant products of a mere versifier. The kindest judgments of them were rendered by those who interpreted them according to the naturalism which prevailed at the time of their recovery.

If Ibsen or Gerhard Hauptmann or Maxim Gorki "wallowed in the mire," as critics of that time often termed it, their concern was the accusation of society: they wished to show that bad deeds grew out of a bad milieu. But there is nothing to be felt in Herondas of such reformatory tendencies or of such pedagogical optimism. If he introduces a matchmaking woman, a pimp, lascivious women, a shrewd shoemaker, or a cruel mother, he does not hint by a single word that these in reality might be poor pitiable creatures.

On the other hand, one cannot say that Herondas merely enjoys the truthful representation of lively "slices of daily life," as did Theocritus in some of his poems. For Herondas people are thoroughly trashy, and sometimes he underlines this concept by contrasts.

I provide only one example, the especially unpleasant third mime, *The Schoolmaster*. A mother brings her son, a true rascal, to his teacher so that he may be thoroughly flogged. Two of his fellow pupils have to hold him, and he is ruthlessly thrashed. But when even the teacher thinks the boy has had enough, the mother urges that the drubbing continue. This is no longer a whipping one can laugh at, like the one which Thersites received or the kind we encountered in comedy. It is only disgusting.

Things that are morally shocking in Herondas come to the fore so crudely that one cannot deny the importance of morality for him. But his work is distinctive in that it never gives the slightest hint of judgment on moral issues—whether he pardons immorality for social or psychological reasons, or whether he lays responsibility on the gods, nature, circumstances, or chance. He merely has his characters speak and act as they are, without bothering about anything else. From the whole of Greek literature I cannot adduce another example of this attitude. Crime, sin, and guilt have always existed in Greek myths and poetry. But the poets always tried to cope with the evil, to investigate its origin and its consequence, and to pass judgment on it.

There have been only two great poets among the Greeks for whom moral problems were not vital, and these are Herondas' contemporaries, Callimachus and Theocritus. They are morally neutral, so to speak, much more than even Menander is. Their characters, who are not particularly good, have human inadequacies of a kind that provoke smiles rather than indignation.

Now the people in Herondas are offensive not because they are criminals but simply because they are vulgar, brutal, and absymally common. They lack exactly those qualities in which Callimachus and Theocritus excelled: education, wit, and sentiment. One must suppose that Herondas came to his own peculiar interpretation of men—with Sophron and Hipponax, who in several respects have been his models, these things look different—because he wished to argue against his two contemporaries and their pretentious poetry.

In any case, he says clearly enough in his poems: all these educated, witty, sentimental pretenses are fraudulent. It is clear that Herondas continues certain ideas of Euripides by furthering the disillusionment and the unmasking of values. But if Eteocles disposed of the moral conventions as mere talk and pronounced the will to power as true reality, nevertheless it was important to him that somebody who felt superior to his fellow men should lay claim upon tyranny. The princes in the *Iphigenia in Aulis,* though disillusioned, still knew what they really ought to be, even though this high claim no longer corresponded to reality. And Aristophanes made it appear as though reasonable and natural life would be restored once the *alazónes,* the vain prattlers, had been checked. For Herondas life is only stupid, rude, and brutal. Even the egotism in which all his characters live has become miserable. Their actions no longer make any sense.

It cannot be denied that this criticism by Herondas reveals something pertinent in the poetry of Callimachus and Theocritus, or to phrase it more cautiously, that he would reveal something if he actually criticized them. Art as an end in itself is in fact something artificial. Such an artificiality—namely, that something has become an end in itself although originally it served another purpose—is found in different places in the civilization of this time. It has been mentioned that with Menander society becomes pure society and no longer pursues common interests or aims except that of living together in peace; also that morals become moral psychology: higher tasks disappear and one goal remains— understanding oneself and others so that everyone can adapt himself to society and so that everyone can have respect and tolerance. Even the importance of psychology shows that the major interests in thinking and feeling are no longer the objectives of truth and beauty, but instead psychological reactions—which means again that what once served as an aim now achieves significance in its own right. If among the Hellenistic poets erudition and education is their special pride, the principle is the same: knowledge enjoys itself. This can be shown in many other respects. Callimachus, for instance, in his love poems does not praise, as Sappho did, the beauty of a beloved person; nor does he actually try to win love, as Anacreon did; but he speaks only of his erotic desires. And surely in Herondas people have nothing but sexual drives.

It is indeed an artificial world in which Callimachus and Theocritus lived. But that does not say by any means that Herondas in exposing this was simply and generally true. Quite the opposite! Whoever says that everything artificial is a lie and ought to be supplanted by something natural fails to recognize that all human civilization is essentially artificial from its very beginning. Therefore what Herondas puts before our eyes is pure barbarism and scarcely rises above bestiality. History itself has passed this judgment. Herondas became almost forgotten. But Callimachus and Theocritus have had a decisive influence on the poetry and thought of subsequent ages down to the eighteenth century. And when at that time Rousseau, the German *Sturm und Drang* movement, and Romanticism recalled the unartificial nature, not only was the way opened for new great poetry but a new barbarism was also made possible. We feel that influence right down to our day.

The radical desire to be natural is caused by a misunderstanding that the abyss we feel to exist between ourselves and the absolute is an arbitrary invention of intellectuals. If we retire with consequent honesty to our own shore, we must be prepared "to be more beastly than every beast," as Mephistopheles says.

The possibilities of Greek poetry were exhausted when the nihilism of Herondas was reached. The ancient Greeks afterward found no essentially new forms. This might give rise to dreary deliberations and the pessimistic view that great and beautiful things arose in the world and without meaning disappeared again. But why should we assert that poetry is the only great accomplishment? Times that have not been fertile in poetry have produced other intellectual achievements, and no century following the Greeks has failed to produce something important in the further development of civilization. And then new poetry has also sprung up again. In this process the original function of Greek poetry has again and again proved its validity. The Muses were the children of Mnemosyne. Poetry has kept alive the memory of some important stations in our intellectual development and by doing so has created a tradition which men have ever since been able to recollect and from which have always again been able to learn and to understand themselves.

INDEX

Aeschylus, 41, 73, 75–77, 79ff., 89;
  Agamemnon, 75ff.; *Hoplon Krisis*,
  41; *Isthmiastai*, 77ff.; *Suppliant
  Maidens*, 75
agathós, 13, 50ff.
aidōs, 73ff.
alazónes, 95, 98, 109
Alcaeus, 29–34, 38, 62, 84; works cited,
  30, 31, 33, 51
Alcman, works cited, 60, 65
Anacreon, 33, 56
andreía, 36
anèr agathós, 13, 50
anthropos, 96ff.
aphrētōr, 6

Apollonius of Rhodes, 103ff.; *Argo-
  nautica*, 104
Aratus, 103ff.
Archilochus, 28–30, 33ff., 58, 60, 84;
  works cited, 24, 29, 38, 61
areté, 13, 56, 61, 64, 69, 78, 80, 83
Aristophanes, 93–96, 98, 100, 109;
  Birds, 94ff.; *Clouds*, 95; *Frogs*, 95
Aristotle, 40, 83; *Politics*, 31
athémistos, 6

Bacchylides, 56–63; *Cassandra*, 59;
  Leucippides, The, 59; poem on
  Marpessa, 58; sixteenth dithyramb,
  53; other works cited, 59, 60, 61, 63

beauty, 47
Benedict, Ruth, 73n.

Callimachus, 57, 64, 102–106, 108–
    110; *Aitia*, 57

democracy, 39
demos, 38
dlandlcha mermerlzeln, 25
dithyramb, 59
Dodds, E. R., v, 73 and n., 74, 80
doulosýne, 42

echthrós, 4, 21ff.
Ehrenberg, Victor, 1n.
Eleusinians, 48
Empedocles, 69–71; works cited, 71
enemy, 20–22, 32, 34, 43
ēnorée, 36
ereundi, 64
eschatiá, 22, 31
Euripides, 73, 79–90, 92, 95–97; *Al-
    cestis*, 83–86; *Antiope*, 41, 79ff.;
    Heracles, 86–89; *Iphigenia in Aulis*,
    89ff., 97, 105, 108; *Orestes*, 88;
    Phoenician Women, 82, 85; other
    work cited (perhaps *Antiope*), 81
ex-, 22

fairy tales, 22
Finley, M. I., 1n., 23
Fränkel, Hermann, v, 9ff.
freedom, 42
friend, 8, 12, 20–23, 27, 29, 31–34,
    43ff., 83–88
Fritz, K. von, 85

Gellius, Aulus, 90n.
geras, 14
god (s), 22, 39, 47, 88, 92, 97
Goethe, Johann W., 27, 101; *Iphi-*

genia, 27; *Faust* (Mephistopheles),
    110
Gorki, Maxim, 107
guest-friend, 22, 55
guilt (conscience), 88, 89
guilt-culture, 79

Hauptmann, Gerhard, 107
hekōn, 51, 52
Herodotus, 30n.
Herondas, 106–110; *The Schoolmas-
    ter*, 107
Hesiod, 39, 51, 76ff.; *Theogony*, 52;
    Works and Days, 76ff.
hetairos, 30–34
historía, 81
Homer, 4–30, 34–37, 45, 56ff., 62,
    64, 76ff., 91ff.; *Aethiopis*, 40; *Iliad*,
    6, 7, 14, 15, 16, 17, 18, 19, 24, 36,
    37, 55, 76; *Odyssey*, 4, 7, 9, 14, 18,
    19, 21, 24, 26, 27, 60
homóphron, *homophronéein*, *homo-
    phrosýne*, 19ff.
honor, 14, 25, 29
Horace, 33
Humboldt, W. von, 11

Ibsen, Henrik, 107
Ibycus, 54–56
inner conflict, 24, 25

Johansen, K. F., 59 and n.
justice, 39ff., 41ff.

language, 10ff.
logos, 84, 97
loneliness, 24–27, 46, 90
love, 8, 12, 21, 109

Marie Antoinette, 106
marriage, 19, 21, 83–86

Menander, 96–102; *Dyscolos*, 96–99; *Epitrepontes*, 101–102
metanoia, 77
mētis, 71
Meton, 94, 95
mime, 106ff.
Mimnermus, 50
mind, active, in Homer, 13; in Pindar, 68
mind, common, in Homer, 13ff., 23ff.
Mnemosyne, 45
mysteries, 47
myths, Pindar, 67, 68; Euripides, 85

New Comedy, 96ff.
Nietzsche, Friedrich, 83
nobility, 31–33
noos, 19, 46, 68

oath, 29ff.
Orphics, 48
orthôs, 84

Parmenides, 69–71, 75, 85; works cited, 70, 71
Petrarch, 3
phalanx, 37
Pheidon, 35
philanthropy, 101
philos, 4, 8ff., 21ff., 83–88
philosophical schools, 48
phrenes, 17
phyái, 63
Pindar, 40, 55–71, 74, 76, 78–81, 85, 92, 104; *Epinicia*, 69; *Isthmian*, 60; *Nemean*, 65, 66; *Olympian*, 53, 63, 65, 67; *Paean*, 57, 61, 64; *Parthenia*, 61; *Pythian*, 60, 65, 66; other works cited, 59, 61, 64, 65, 68, 93
Pittacus, 29ff., 35, 51
Plato, *Gorgias*, 79, 80, 82, 83; *Pro-tagoras*, 50; *Republic*, 83, 94; *Theaetetus*, 81, 82
polis, 37, 38
Polycrates, 54ff.
ponos, 64
primitive society, 10ff., 22
progress, 91
psyche, 10, 80
psychology, 92, 100
Pythagoreans, 48

Rousseau, Jean Jacques, 12, 110

Sappho, 15, 44–47, 60, 62, 85; works cited, 41, 44, 45, 47, 50
Schwartz, Eduard, 90n.
Semonides, 78
Seven Sages, the, 35
Shakespeare, William, 3
shame-culture, 73ff., 83
Simonides, 69ff.; drinking song to the Thessalian Skopas, 50–52; victory song, 53; other works cited, 51, 53, 58
slavery, 42
slaves, 41, 105
Socrates, 95ff.
Solon, 35, 38–43, 50, 52, 62, 69ff.; *Elegy to the Muses*, 38, 39, 43; other works cited, 40, 42, 82
soma, 10
sophia, 64, 69, 96, 104
Sophocles, 73, 89; *Oedipus Rex*, 77
state, the, 37ff.
Stesichorus, 62; works cited, 55n., 60n., 65n.
syn-, 23ff., 32, 87
synesis, 88

Theocritus, 103–106, 108, 110; *Idylls*, 105

Theognis, 34
Theophrastus, 99
Thersites, 14, 100
Thucydides, work cited, 77
thymos, 9ff., 15–19, 21, 30, 36, 40
tīmē, 14
Timocreon, work cited, 58
tyrant, 30, 33, 42
Tyrtaeus, 17ff., 35–38, 40, 50, 62, 69ff., 80; battle songs, 36, 37, 78

unanimity, 14–21

virtue, 13ff., 36, 56, 61, 64, 69, 78, 97
vita activa et contemplativa, 82
Voigt, Eva M., 44n.

whipping, 14, 94, 100, 107
Wilamowitz-Moellendorff, Ulrich von, 22 and n.

Xenophanes, 66, 69ff.; works cited, 70, 81
xynōnie, 28; *xynón agathón*, 37